THE QUEST FOR SUMER

Leonard Cottrell

THE QUEST
FOR SUMER

G. P. PUTNAM'S SONS
NEW YORK

To
the memory
of my good friend,
MOHAMMED ZAKARIA GONEIM

CONTENTS

ILLUSTRATIONS
Following page 96

ACKNOWLEDGEMENTS

Acknowledgements and thanks are due to Macmillan & Co. Ltd. for permission to quote from *Amurath to Amurath* by Gertrude Bell; to John Murray Ltd. for the extract from *By Nile and Tigris* by Sir Wallis Budge; to Routledge & Kegan Paul Ltd. for the extract from *New Light on the Most Ancient East* by Gordon Childe; to Ernest Benn Ltd. for the extracts from *Excavations at Ur, Development of Sumerian Art, Ur of the Chaldees* and *Birth of Civilisation in the Near East,* all by Sir Leonard Woolley; to T. & T. Clarke for the extract from *Explorations in Bible Lands* by H. V. Hilprecht; to Thames & Hudson Ltd. for the extracts from *History begins at Sumer* by S. N. Kramer; to the Oxford University Press for the extracts from *Twin Rivers* and *Foundations in the Dust,* both by Seton Lloyd; to Peter Davies Ltd. for the extract from *Mesopotamia* by Seton Lloyd; to Falcon Wing Press for the extracts from *The Tablets of Sumer* by S. N. Kramer; to the University of Chicago Press for the extract from *The Intellectual Adventure* (Copyright 1946 by The University of Chicago); to Princeton University Press for the extracts from *Ancient Near Eastern Texts* by J. B. Pritchard.

INTRODUCTION

"And the beginning of his kingdom was Babel, and Accad, and Calneh, in the land of Shinar" (GENESIS 10: 10).

So the author of Genesis describes the realm of Nimrod "the Archer", that far-off, shadowy king whose figure looms, dim but giant-like, out of the mists which shroud the beginnings of recorded history. Was he God or man? Reality or legend? Or something of both? He was man enough to defy God, for when it thundered and lightened, Nimrod would shoot his arrows into the sky in defiance of the deity who caused the storm. And when one of his arrows returned to earth damp with a liquid resembling blood, Nimrod rejoiced, saying that he had fought the God successfully, and wounded him. Like another Sumerian hero, Gilgamesh, he epitomised defiant humanity, shaking his fist at the sky and daring Nature to destroy him.

According to Moslem historians, Nimrod was the son of Cush; he built the citadel of Birs and is supposed to have reigned 500 years. "In his reign the worship of the stars and of fire appeared upon the earth." He disputed on theology with Abraham, and, when he felt he was getting the worst of the argument, shut the Patriarch up in a fiery oven, from which he was miraculously rescued. Earlier, when astrologers, reading the horoscope of the year in which Abraham was to be born, observed that the child would eventually destroy their religion, Nimrod promptly ordered all the newborn babies to be killed. But Abraham's mother hid the child in a cave and he escaped.

When God took Abraham under his protection, and his religion flourished, Nimrod built a great tower so that he might ascend it and see Abraham's God. Failing in this, he had himself borne aloft in a chest by four huge birds, but when the strength of the birds failed the chest fell to earth, causing a mighty earthquake. Finally, after a battle between the followers of Nimrod and Abraham, the Patriarch's God sent down fire from heaven, destroyed the great tower built by Nimrod and confounded the speech of his followers. As retribution, God sent an insect which crawled into Nimrod's head, and caused him to suffer agony for several centuries before he died, a mighty king destroyed by one of the smallest of God's creatures.

Observant readers will have noted that this ancient legend contains elements of (a) the story of Shadrach, Mesech and Abednego at the court of Nebuchadnezzar, (b) Herod's Massacre of the Innocents and the escape of Jesus Christ, (c) the Greek myth of the Flight of Icarus and (d) the Biblical story of the Tower of Babel. There is also, in Nimrod's defiance of the Sky-God, something which recalls the stubborn pride of the Homeric heroes who also challenged the omnipotent Gods. When to this, one adds the fact that southern Mesopotamia was the legendary site of the Garden of Eden and that Sumerian literature contains a description of a great Flood and the building of an Ark, the least imaginative among us may ask, "Was this where it all began? Are Sumeriologists right in calling southern Mesopotamia 'The Cradle of Mankind'?"

Possibly; we still do not know. The very existence of a Sumerian civilisation was not recognised until about seventy years ago; and even today, after three generations of archaeologists have shone the light of their learnings on this unattractive corner of the earth, far less is known about Sumer than about the great riverine civilisation of Ancient Egypt. Egyptologists and Sumeriologists still dispute which civilisation arose first; whether it was beside the Nile or the Euphrates that men first learned to organise themselves into settled communities, develop arts and industries, became literate and began the historical process of which we are the latest (but, let us hope, not the final) product.

The home of the Sumerians, the "Land of Shinar", is now known. It can be identified on a map of modern Iraq. Its cities, formerly only Biblical names, have been identified and excavated; Ur of the Chaldees, Lagash, Accad, Calneh, Nippur, Eridu, Uruk, and many others, are no longer mere mounds of crumbling brick between the Tigris and the Euphrates. We now know a great deal about the people who lived in them, four, five, six thousand years ago; about how they dressed, how they lived, the food they ate, the songs they sang, the gods they worshipped and the buildings they erected. Yet, in a curious way they still remain detached, in a manner that the Ancient Egyptians do not. To the present writer at least the Pharaoh Rameses II is more real and accessible than, say, Naram-Sin. Thebes has more solidity than Ur, and the Egyptian love-goddess, Hathor, seems more approachable than her Sumerian equivalent, Inanna, even when a Sumerian poet writes of her:

> *"The wig of her forehead she has taken. . . .*
> *Small lapis stones she has fastened about her neck,*
> *Sparkling stones she has fastened to her breast. . . .*
> *Kohl (with which) she has daubed her eyes*
> *With the gala-garment, the garment of ladyship,*
> *She has covered her body. . . ."*

Even if one knew nothing of the antiquity of Ancient Egypt and was totally unaware of her achievements in social organisation, art and science, one glance at the portrait-bust of Tuthmosis III, Nefrititi or the slim wife of Ramose, sitting, eternally poised and elegant, at a banquet in her husband's tomb, is enough to establish a warm human contact. For the writer this is not true of the Sumerians. Those rigid, archaic figures with their large hooked noses and eyes enlarged to an unnatural prominence, the stiff folds of the robes, the shrewd mercantile stare from the faces of gods and men alike discourage contact. These people are vigorously alive, but the life they exhibit is one into which I find it difficult to enter. Yet their very remoteness makes them even more fascinating. One peers at their figures behind the glass cases of a museum —in London, Berlin or Damascus—hoping for a clue. The protruberant eyes stare back and one retires, defeated.

Yet their poetic literature has a power and a sweep which is and can be overwhelming. "The Story of Gilgamesh" has a Homeric vitality and splendour. How can we relate such figures as Gilgamesh, who hacked down vast forests, and Nimrod, who fired his arrows into the face of God, with the self-complacent wide-eyed little statues which confront us in our galleries? This to me is one of the paradoxes of Sumer.

There are many excellent books on Sumerian art, literature, religion and the excavation of Sumerian sites. I have read a number of these, have talked with Sumerologists and once paid an all-too-fleeting visit to southern Iraq. But I am still far more at home in Egypt, Greece and Crete than in "The Land of Shinar". Perhaps these very limitations, lamentable in a scholar, may help to establish a sympathetic bond with the reader who is similarly perplexed. I hope so, because most authors and all actors like to know their audience. I imagine mine to contain many people like myself, interested in the ancient world, fairly familiar with the civilisation of the Eastern Mediterranean, but anxious to learn more about that lesser-known culture which grew from the lower Tigris and Euphrates.

This book is a journey through both space and time. Sometimes we shall look down on Iraq from a jet aircraft, skimming across the featureless plain which was once the most fertile land on earth. At other times we shall see the same country through the eyes of nineteenth-century travellers, who explored it on foot, on horseback and on those enormous rafts called *keleks*, made of timber and inflated skins, which still glide down the great rivers from Mosul to the Persian Gulf. We shall delve underground, too, in a test pit driven through the successive strata of a buried city which has known forty centuries of occupation. We shall stand on the lofty peak of a *ziggurat*, one of those tiered towers from which the Chaldaean priests made their dawn offerings to Enlil or Inanna, and see far below us the dry, dusty ridges which mark the course of long-vanished irrigation canals.

We shall meet heroes like Gilgamesh, who was beloved of the goddess Ishtar and who fought and defeated the gods of forest and storm. We shall see beauty, in the exquisitely-fashioned gold and jewelled head-dress of Queen Shub-Ad, and in the delicate, jewel-like mosaics of the columned wall at Warka. Horror is present, too, in the macabre death-pits at Ur, in which some five thousand years ago, court ladies, attendants and soldiers lay down in the earth and surrendered their lives so that their rulers might be suitably attended in the world beyond the tomb.

Experiences such as these have been made possible only through the labours of three generations of scholars. But in order to appreciate them to the full we have to contribute something ourselves—imagination. For in Sumeria there are few monuments to capture the eye with an obvious appeal. There is no Sumerian equivalent of the Egyptian Pyramids, the Temple of Karnak, the Valley of the Kings, or the Palace of Knossos. There are only the two great rivers, rolling sluggishly across a flat, dun-coloured expanse, sun-scorched throughout most of the year, but turning into a malarial swamp during the brief but violent periods of storm and flood.

Here and there, rising out of the plain, are the "tells"— mounds of crumbling mud-brick and broken pottery— which are all that is left of the proud cities of ancient Sumer. The kingly chronicles, the epic poetry, the letters and documents, are rarely inscribed on stone monuments, and never on rolls of papyrus; they have survived in thousands of small baked-clay tablets which look as impressive as dog-biscuits, and which were quite valueless until the *cuneiform* writing

inscribed on them was deciphered. The lovely Sumerian pottery is rarely found intact; the golden goblets, crowns and
jewellery found at Ur are rare, and precious examples of
Sumerian craftsmanship are miraculously preserved in a few
intact tombs which have escaped robbery. There are no
colossal statuary, but some fine sculpture, and a multitude
of those more mundane objects from children's toys to
women's toilet instruments, which speak of the common
humanity we share with those long-dead people.

The explorers, archaeologists, linguists who, over one
hundred years, have gradually revealed the glory of ancient
Sumer are interesting people in themselves. Some of them—
particularly the pioneers such as Rich, Layard and Loftus—
faced greater dangers and hardships and wrote more vividly
of them than their more scientific modern successors. I have
therefore drawn liberally on their own accounts in preparing
the first part of this book, which tries to show how the long-
forgotten civilisation of lower Mesopotamia was discovered
and interpreted. The second part shows how the rich and
abundant literature of Sumer—myths and legends, chronicles
and "King-Lists", religious texts, legal and business documents—enabled archaeologists to identify the buried cities,
interpret objects and monuments, and partly reconstruct the
political and social history of Sumer. The third part examines
but does not hazard a definite answer to a number of fascinating problems. Who were the Sumerians? Where did they
come from? What did they look like, and what kind of life
did they live? And what brought about their downfall?

Running through, and, I hope, illuminating the text, is
the fourth and perhaps most important element, the art of
Sumer, which the reader must assess for himself from
the illustrations, which have been carefully selected to
counterpoint my theme. Pictures are sometimes more evoca-
tive than words; to some readers the illustrations may convey a more direct message than the text. I hope so, for in this
journey both of us—reader and author—are explorers.

LEONARD COTTRELL

CHAPTER ONE

EARLY EXPLORERS

THE discovery of the land of Sumer and its people was slow and gradual; it was also, in the early stages, accidental. In this the Sumerian culture differs from that of Egypt. Although the civilisation of Ancient Egypt died some two thousand years ago, its existence has never been forgotten. Successive conquerors, Romans, Arabs, Turks, imposed their own cultures on the ancient land, but they could not—even had they wished—obliterate the titanic monuments left by their predecessors; the Pyramids, the temples and the thousands of inscribed and painted tombs which cluster beside the Nile from the Delta to the Sudanese border. But Sumer, like Mycenean Greece, was utterly lost to knowledge for several thousand years.

The reasons for this are partly geographical and partly political. First, lower Mesopotamia, of which Sumer formed part, is a vast plain of alluvial mud brought down by the twin rivers, the Tigris and Euphrates. Unlike Egypt, which has an abundance of accessible and easily-worked stone, lower Mesopotamia has none, so that in Sumerian times buildings were almost entirely of mud-brick, either sun-dried or kiln-baked. When stone was needed it had to be brought from a great distance and was therefore used very sparingly. It is true that mud-brick buildings have survived for five thousand years in Egypt, but that country is not subject, as is Mesopotamia, to violent rainstorms, floods and sandstorms which rapidly erode the mud-brick buildings once a city has been deserted.

Secondly, Egypt was protected by well-defined frontiers; the Mediterranean on the north, the deserts on east and west. The only threat was from Nubia in the south, but, although the Nubians once conquered Egypt in a time of decadence, the Pharaohs usually succeeded in keeping their southern neighbours in check. Mesopotamia, however, enjoys no such protection; the country is open on all sides, and thus has had to endure a succession of invasions from the north and east. These invaders, after ravaging and killing, usually built afresh on the ruins of the cities they had destroyed (or partly destroyed). Thus Mesopotamia resembles a palimpsest on which a number of peoples have written their names one above the other. And right at the bottom, over-written by Elamites, Babylonians, Assyrians, Persians, Arabs, Mongols, lies Sumer.

A third reason for the late discovery of Sumer is that, until fairly recently, Mesopotamia was not easily accessible to Europeans. A hundred years ago there were only two ways of reaching it, on horseback over the dangerous overland route from the east Mediterranean coast, or through Turkey and Armenia; or by the long sea journey round Africa to Basrah on the Persian Gulf. Even if one reached Basrah there was still a journey of many weeks, mainly on horseback, before one reached Baghdad and Mosul.

Mr. Seton Lloyd, in his book *Mesopotamia*, points out that

> Sir Wallis Budge, who went on behalf of the British Museum, had a Turkish inspector sent from Istanbul to supervise his work at Nineveh, and this gentleman, being unable even to ride a donkey, was compelled to travel the entire distance in a "Takh tarawan", an elementary wooden litter slung between a pair of mules. As one might expect, he arrived more dead than alive.[1]

Add to such difficulties the presence of hostile Bedouin

[1] Lloyd, Seton. *Mesopotamia*, Lovat Dickson, London, 1936.

tribesmen, a summer heat of 120° in the shade, the threat of typhoid and other diseases, and it is hardly surprising that, when Egypt was already well-charted territory to Europeans, they tended to shun Mesopotamia.

And yet, from the twelfth century onwards, a trickle of European visitors did visit the Land of the Two Rivers, and described it. Benjamin of Tudela, a learned Spanish Jew, travelled to Mosul seven hundred years ago and had no difficulty in identifying Nineveh. "This city," he writes, "situated on the Tigris, is connected with ancient Nineveh by a bridge." It is true Nineveh lies now in utter ruins, but numerous villages and small towns occupy its former space. The German, Leonhart Rauwolff, in 1575, refers to a "high round hill" outside the city.

It is entirely honeycombed, [he says], being inhabited by poor people, whom I often saw crawling out and in in large numbers, like ants in their heap. At that place and in the region hereabouts years ago the mighty city of Nineveh was situated.

And Sir Antony Shirley, in the time of Queen Elizabeth I of England, speaks of

Nineve, that which God Himself calleth That great Citie, hath not one stone standing which may give memory of the being of a towne. One English mile from it is a place called Mosul, a small thing, rather to be a witnesse of the other's mightinesse and God's judgement, than of any fashion of magnificence in itselfe.

"... God's judgement." One consistent thread runs through all these descriptions by ancient travellers—that of Old Testament prophecy. No matter for what purpose Christians visited Mesopotamia, whether it was diplomacy or commerce, they could not fail to be interested in the remains of cities such as Nineveh and Babylon which, according to the Scriptures, were destroyed by God's wrath. Pietro della Valle, an Italian nobleman, John Cartwright, an Englishman, and Tavernier, a German of the seventeenth century,

all add their testimony. Pietro della Valle was the first to
examine the real site of Babylon, and carried back with him a
few inscribed bricks from Babil, which he visited in 1616. He
describes "Babil", the northern-most mound of the ruins of
Babylon, as "the most remarkable thing I ever saw", a huge
rectangular tower or pyramid with its corners pointing to the
four cardinal points. The Abbé de Beauchamp, who was the
Pope's Vicar-General of Babylonia between 1780 and 1790,
twice visited Babylon and described "an elevation which is
flat on the top, of an irregular form, and intersected by
ravines". He also took back specimens of those curious mud-
bricks inscribed with writing which, at that time, could not
be understood.

> Important as the report of Beauchamp must appear in the
> light of modern knowledge [writes Hilprecht[1]] . . . it con-
> veyed to the public for the first time a tolerably clear idea
> of the exact position and enormous size of the ruins of
> Babylon and the great possibilities connected with its
> future excavation. It was particularly in England that
> people began to realize the importance of these cylinders
> and bricks covered with *cuneiform*[2] writing. . . . The East
> India Company of London became the first public ex-
> ponent of this rapidly-growing interest in Great Britain, by
> ordering their Resident at Basra to obtain several speci-
> mens of these remarkable bricks and send them carefully
> packed to London.

It is difficult in our modern, secular civilisation to appreciate the excitement which was aroused in nineteenth-
century Europe by the news, filtering through from the
Middle East, that the fabulous cities of the Old Testament,
Nineveh and Babylon, could still be identified, and perhaps
excavated. Our Victorian forefathers lived far closer to the
Bible than most of us do today. Every week worshippers

---

[1] Hilprecht, H.V. *Explorations in Bible Lands*, T. and T. Clark, Edinburgh,
1903.

[2] Called *cuneiform* from the wedge-shaped formation of the signs.

heard the splendid prophetic denunciations by the Hebrew prophets intoned from a thousand pulpits . . .

How art thou fallen from Heaven, O Lucifer, son of the morning! How art thou cut down to the ground which didst weaken the nations!

—thundered Isaiah, exulting over the fall of Nineveh and the dreaded Assyrians. "Flocks lie down in the midst of her," prophesied Zephanaiah. "The gates of the rivers shall be opened, and the palace shall be dissolved."
"Woe to the bloody city! It is full of lies and robbery; the prey departeth not." "The noise of the whip, and the noise of the rattling wheels, and the prancing horses, and the jumping chariots." All the pride, arrogance and military might of Assyria is enshrined in that passage from Nahum, and so is her desolation in another of his prophecies, a passage soaked in hate of the oppressor.

Thy shepherds slumber, O king of Assyria; thy nobles shall dwell in the dust; thy people is scattered upon the mountains, and no man gathereth them.
There is no healing of thy bruise; thy wound is grievous; all that hear the bruit of thee clap their hands over thee; for upon whom hath not thy wickedness passed continually?

And who had not heard of Babylon the Great, whose very name had become a symbol of pride, wealth, luxury and vice, the city to which the Jews were carried into captivity, when

A voice was heard in Ramah, lamentations, and bitter weeping; Rachel weeping for her children, refused to be comforted for her children, because they were not. . . .

It is somewhat ironical that to millions of us in the mid-twentieth century these words have a bitter contemporary reality, which few men of the nineteenth century would appreciate; for we, unlike most of them, have also heard the "sound of the whip...and the rattling wheels" and "Rachel weeping for her children". But to our great-grandfathers the appeal of these words was partly religious and partly romantic. And if it is objected that this has little to do with Sumer, I can reply that it was the prophetic literature of the Old Testament which first led Europeans to investigate the great mounds of Asshur, Nineveh and Babylon; and that these excavations led in turn to the gradual revelation of that far older civilisation which had flourished beside the lower Tigris and Euphrates long before Abraham settled in the land of Shinar.

CHAPTER TWO

A NEW LIGHT ON THE ANCIENT EAST

Most of the men who explored "the Bible lands" in the first half of the nineteenth century took the words of the Old Testament literally. When they had identified or thought they had identified the Tower of Babel, they searched diligently for signs of the fire which God sent down from heaven to destroy that monument of idolatry. For instance, Sir Robert Ker Porter, who travelled in the Middle East between 1817 and 1820, and who visited Babylon, wrote

> It does not seem improbable that what we now see on the fire-blasted summit of the pile, its rent wall and scattered fragments with their purely vitrified masses, may be a part of that very stage of the primeval tower which felt the effects of Divine vengeance.

A few days later, when this explorer paid a second visit to the site, he was rewarded by the sight of "three majestic lions taking the air upon the heights of the pyramid" and promptly refers his readers to the passage in Isaiah which prophecies that "Wild beasts of the desert shall lie there; and their houses shall be full of doleful creatures".[1]

It is easy to sneer at pious credulity, but in fact the Bible is a reliable, indeed essential, guide to the ancient civilisations of Mesopotamia, particularly when interpreted in the

[1] Isaiah 13: 21.

light of archaeological knowledge. If it was the comparatively late Assyrian and Babylonian cities which first drew explorers to the area, this was only an accident of geography. Nineveh and Khorsobad are accessible from Mosul, and Babylon from Baghdad. Also when explorers such as Layard, Botta and de Sarzec dug into these colossal mounds they were rewarded by finding huge sculptures and bas-reliefs of terrifying power and majesty, which had once adorned the palaces of the Assyrian kings. When these winged lions and bulls, processional and battle-scenes, were transported with great difficulty to Europe, they caused such excitement that for many years archaeologists concentrated on the cities of northern Mesopotamia, practically to the exclusion of the flat, desolate southern plain.

Earlier in the nineteenth century, when Iraq formed part of the Ottoman Empire, regular diplomatic relations had been established between Britain and the Sublime Porte. Consular Agents were appointed at Mosul and Baghdad, usually young men of education who occupied their leisure in exploration and occasionally a little amateur excavation. Among these was Claudius Rich, who had been Resident of the East India Company in Baghdad. Lord Byron refers to him in his poem *Don Juan*:

> *Though Claudius Rich, Esquire, some bricks has got*
> *And written lately two memoirs upon't.*

Rich explored the mounds of Nineveh more systematically than his predecessors, and published valuable memoirs of his investigations, with maps and plans. His ardent, romantic spirit responded strongly to Iraq, and his writing vividly catches the atmosphere of the country. Here he describes his first sight of the great *ziggurat*[1] of *Birs Nimrud*:

> The morning was at first stormy, and threatened a severe fall of rain, but as we approached the object of our journey, the heavy clouds separating, discovered the *Birs* frowning over the plain, and presenting the appearance of a circular

[1] Tiered tower of which many examples exist.

hill, crowned by a tower, with a high ridge extending along the foot of it. It being entirely concealed from our view, during the first part of our ride, prevented us from acquiring the gradual idea, in general so prejudicial in effect, and so particularly lamented by those who visit the Pyramids. Just as we were within the proper distance, it burst at once about our sight, in the midst of rolling masses of black clouds partially obscured by that kind of haze whose indistinctness is one great cause of sublimity, while a few strong catches of stormy light, thrown upon the desert in the background, served to give some idea of the immense and dreary solitude of the wastes in which this venerable ruin stands.

The same romantic feeling for landscape appears in the writings of a later explorer, William Kennet Loftus, who writes thus of Warka, an ancient Sumerian city which he visited in the fifties.

The desolation and solitude of Warka are even more striking than the scene presented by Babylon itself. There is no life for miles around. No river glides in grandeur at the base of its mounds, no green dates flourish near its ruins. The jackal and the hyena appear to shun the dull aspect of its tombs. The king of birds never hovers over its deserted wastes. A blade of grass, or an insect, finds no existence there. The shrivelled lichen alone, clinging to the weathered surface of the broken brick, seems to glory in its universal dominion over these barren walls. Of all the desolate pictures I have ever beheld, that of Warka incomparably surpasses all.

And:

I know nothing more exciting or impressive than the first sight of one of those great Chaldaean piles looming in solitary grandeur from the surrounding plains and marshes. A thousand thoughts and surmises concerning its past eventful history and origin—its gradual rise and rapid fall—naturally present themselves to the mind of the spectator. The hazy atmosphere of early morning is peculiarly favourable to considerations and impressions of this character, and the gray mist intervening between the gazer and the object of his reflections, imparts to it a dreamy existence. This fairy-like effect is further heightened by mirage, which strangely and fantastically magnifies its form, elevating it from the ground, and causing it to dance and quiver in the rarefied air.

In the thirty odd years which divide Rich from Loftus, a tremendous stride had been taken towards a fuller understanding of ancient Mesopotamia, the partial decipherment of the mysterious *cuneiform* writing which had puzzled generations of scholars. The feat was accomplished by two scholars, working quite independently, but whereas one of them, Colonel Sir Henry Creswicke Rawlinson, an English Orientalist, won great acclaim in his own lifetime, the other, a young German teacher named Georg Friederich Grotefend, was prevented by academic snobbery from enjoying the recognition his work deserved. In 1802, when only 27 years of age, Grotefend solved the riddle in practically a few days, thirty-three years before Rawlinson.

Under the magical touch of his hand [writes Hilprecht] the mystic and complicated characters of ancient Persia suddenly gained new life. But when he was far enough advanced to announce to the Academy of Sciences at Gottingen the epoch-making discovery which established his fame and reputation forever, that learned body, though composing men of eminent mental training and intelligence, strange to say, declined to publish the Latin memoirs of this little-known college teacher, who did not belong to the University circle proper. It was not until ninety years later (1893) that his original papers were re-discovered and published. . . .[1]

[1] Hilprecht, H.V. *Explorations in Bible Lands*, T. and T. Clark, Edinburgh, 1903.

As this epochal discovery bears directly on the revelation of ancient Sumer, I hope I may be excused a brief quotation from my book *The Lost Pharaohs* in which Grotefend's achievement is summarised

> He noticed that on a certain cuneiform tablet the same set of symbols occurred repeatedly in successive lines. It occurred to him that this might be a chronological list of the Persian Kings and that the recurrent symbols might represent the words "the son of" thus part of the inscription might read

>> "(A) the son of
>> (B) the son of
>> (C) the son of
>> (D) etc. (A, B, C, D, representing the Kings)"

Naturally Grotefend was familiar with the chronology of the Archemenid kings (of Persia) so he tried putting their names to the symbols A, B, C, and D. He knew that one of the kings should be Xerxes, which was a great help, as the King had two "X" sounds to his name which should be represented by the same cuneiform symbol. To his delight he found that the lines (B) and (D) *did* contain two similar symbols in the position where they should occur if the name were indeed Xerxes. Now there were two kings named Xerxes in the Archemenid Dynasty. Therefore, if (B) and (D) each represented XerXes, (A) must represent Darius, son of Xerxes II, (C) must be Artaxerxes I, father of Xerxes II, and (E) must signify Darius I, father of the first Xerxes. Thus the inscription might read

>> "(A) Darius II the son of
>> (B) Xerxes II the son of
>> (C) Artaxerxes I the son of
>> (D) Xerxes I the son of
>> (E) Darius I"

In each case Grotefend found that the cuneiform signs were identical where the same names should have occurred, and so, bit by bit he was able to establish the phonetic equivalents of a number of cuneiform signs. This, of course was only the beginning. . . .[1]

Thus an inspired guess followed by years of laborious research enabled a young obscure scholar to let a great light into the ancient East. Fortunately Grotefend's work, though unpublished by his University, was circulated to other linguists, so that news of this great historical event spread throughout the learned Europe. A little later, in far-off Persia, a young British army officer solved the same problem, almost independently, by a similar process of combination and substitution. Colonel (later Sir Henry) Rawlinson, who was knighted for his achievements, was one of those remarkable Englishmen for whom the East has such a powerful attraction that they settle there, become Oriental scholars, and often contrive to exert a greater moral influence than the nominal rulers of the country.

After serving for a time in the Indian Army he got himself posted to Baghdad as British Resident and Consul-General in Baghdad. He was equally distinguished as a soldier, explorer, decipherer and linguist; he deciphered the famous Behistun Rock in Persia, with its cuneiform inscriptions in Elamite, Persian and Babylonian, and corroborated the findings of Grotefend. During his long period in the Residency he was a constant source of help and inspiration to the scholars and explorers of several nationalities who came out to excavate the monuments of Assyria and Babylonia. He worked away steadily at the decipherment of the cuneiform, and

in order to enable himself to continue working in the hot weather, built a little shelter at the bottom of the Residency Garden overlooking the river. Over this little shelter water was pumped continually enabling the great man to work in tolerable comfort even when the temperature of Baghdad rose to 120 degrees in the shade. In this water-

[1] Cottrell, Leonard. *Lost Cities*, Robert Hale, 1957.

cooled study scholars of all nationalities were equally welcome.[1]

Long before the end of the century Rawlinson had become a legend in the Middle East, and, though it does not directly concern Sumer, I cannot resist quoting an anecdote told by Sir E. Wallis Budge who visited Baghdad in the nineties, and talked to an old Turkish official called Ya'kub, who had worked for Rawlinson.

"Pasha," he said to Budge, "I tell you true. The Balios Beg [Rawlinson] lived here for twelve years, and each year his power became stronger. And towards the end of his time, had he taken one dog, and put his English hat on his head, and sent the dog to the *Serai*, all the people in the Bazaar would have made way for him and bowed to him. And the soldiers would have stood still and presented arms to him as he passed. And the officials of the *Serai* would have embraced him. And if he had sent another dog with another of his hats across the river to Kazimen, the Shi-ites and the Sunnites would have stopped fighting each other and would have asked him to take coffee with them."[2]

Ya'kub went on:

"In knowledge and learning the Balios was like God; as a horseman he was like Antar, as a king he was like Nimrod, and when he spoke at the Mijlis [Town Council] of Baghdad the heart of the Wali Pasha melted, and the knees of the Councillors gave way under them."[2]

Budge asked the old man if it was true that on one occasion Rawlinson had knocked together the heads of two Pashas who were quarrelling and holding up business. "Quite true," replied Ya'kub with a reminiscent smile. "That day the Balios was like a lion."

[1] Cottrell, Leonard. *Lost Cities*, Robert Hale, 1957.

[2] Budge, Sir E. Wallis. *By Nile and Tigris*, John Murray, 1920.

CHAPTER THREE

THE TIME-TUNNEL

MANY years ago, in a book on the civilisation of Ancient Egypt, I described how the time-frontier had gradually retreated as archaeologists probed deeper and deeper into the origins of the Nile Valley culture. Perhaps a better simile is a tunnel, brightly lit in places where our knowledge is greatest, dimmer in other sections and finally fading into complete darkness. Then a new discovery is made, light floods our path and we are able to move back for another thousand or more years.

So it was with Mesopotamia. We have seen how the earliest European travellers were attracted to the cities of Assyria and Babylon mentioned by the Old Testament writers, cities whose names had been preserved by local tradition and could therefore be identified, and which were accessible from Baghdad or Mosul. This is why northern Mesopotamia was the first area to be investigated by archaeologists, while the monotonous southern plain, stretching down to the marshy malarial estuaries and the Persian Gulf, was rarely visited. Remote, unhealthy and containing few identifiable monuments, it was left to its desolation. Meanwhile, in the more fruitful north, a succession of explorers dug into the colossal brick-heaps of Nineveh, Khorsobad and Kuyujnik, discovering works of Assyrian art which gripped the imagination of the Victorian public and encouraged the Museums to mount fresh expeditions.

Of these explorers Paul Emile Botta, who discovered the

palace of the Assyrian king Sargon II, was French; Sir Henry Layard, who unearthed the palaces of Ashurbanipal and Ezarhaddon, with their magnificent sculptures, was British. With a Turkish assistant, Christian Rassam, he also dug later in the Palace of Sennacherib, the Assyrian king who is mentioned in the Book of Isaiah, and discovered the great Royal Library of some 26,000 cuneiform documents, some of which contained literature more than two thousand years earlier than Sennacherib. A fourth explorer, Hormudz Rassam, also Turkish, re-opened Nineveh in 1852 and found another great library, that of the Assyrian monarch Ashurbanipal, and the famous "lion-hunt" sculptures which are one of the principal glories of the British Museum.

It is difficult to overestimate the impact which these discoveries made on Europe and the United States in the seventies and eighties of the last century. For the first time archaeological research seemed to confirm, in a most exciting way, the teachings of the Old Testament. Although this has only an indirect bearing on Sumer, it is worth turning aside for a moment to compare two extracts from the Holy Scriptures with parallel statements found among the cuneiform inscriptions discovered in the palaces of Sennacherib and Ashurbanipal.

In Chapter 36 of the Book of Isaiah the Biblical chronicle describes a time when Sennacherib, king of Assyria, made war on Egypt, and the cities of Judah were drawn into the conflict. Hezekiah was then on the throne of Judah.

Now it came to pass in the fourteenth year of king Hezekiah that Sennacherib, king of Assyria, came up against all the defended cities of Judah, and took them. And the king of Assyria sent Rabshekeh from Lachish to Jerusalem unto king Hezekiah with a great army. And he stood by the conduit of the upper pool in the highway of the fuller's field. Then came forth unto him Eliakhim Hikiah's son, which was over the house, and Shebna the scribe, and Joah, Asaph's son, the recorder.

Rebshakeh, the Assyrian commander, then dictated to these Jewish emissaries a message from his royal master, calling upon Hezekiah to abandon his alliance with Egypt.

Lo, thou trustest in the staff of this broken reed, on Egypt; whereon if a man lean, it will go into his hand, and pierce it; so is Pharaoh, king of Egypt to all that trust in him. But if thou say to me, We trust in the Lord our God; is it not he, whose high places and whose altars Hezekiah hath taken away, and said to Judah and to Jerusalem, Ye shall worship before this altar? Now therefore give pledges, I pray thee, to my royal master the king of Assyria, and I will give thee two thousand horses, if thou be able on thy part to set riders upon them. How then will thou turn away the face of one captain of the least of my master's servants and put thy trust in Egypt for chariots and for horsemen.

The sequel is well-known. Eliakhim, Shebna and Joah bore the Assyrian captain's message to Hezekiah, who "rent his clothes and covered himself with sackcloth, and went into the house of the Lord". He sent the messengers on to Isaiah, asking for his advice. Isaiah said:

Thus saith the Lord, Be not afraid of the words that thou hast heard, wherewith the servants of the king of Assyria have blasphemed me. Behold I will send a blast upon him, and he shall hear a rumour, and return to his own land; and I will cause him to fall by the sword in his own land.

In a later verse of the same chapter the Biblical chronicler writes of Sennacherib's making war on "Tirhakah king of Ethiopia", and of how the Assyrian king boasted of the destruction he had inflicted on the cities of Judah.

Behold, thou hast heard what the kings of Assyria have done to all lands by destroying them utterly; and shalt thou be delivered? Have the gods of the nations delivered them which my fathers have destroyed, as Gozn, and Haran, and Reph, and the children of Eden that were in Talassar? Where is the king of Hamath, and the king of

Arphad, and the king of the city of Sepharvaim, Hena and Ivah?

Here is an Assyrian inscription, in cuneiform, on the Prism of Sennacherib, found in that king's palace, and now in the Oriental Institute Museum in Chicago. Sennacherib himself is speaking.

In the continuation of my campaign I besieged Beth-dagon, Joppa, Banai-Barqa, Azuru, cities belonging to Sidqui who did not bow to my feet quickly (enough). I conquered (them) and carried their spoils away. The officials, the patricians, and the (common) people of Ekron—who had thrown Padi, their king, into fetters (because he was) loyal (to) (his) solemn oath (sworn) by the god Ashur, and had handed him over to Hezekiah, the Jew (and) he (Hezekiah) held him in prison, unlawfully as if he (Padi) had been an enemy—he had become afraid and had called for help upon the kings of Egypt (and) the bowmen, the chariot-(corps) and the cavalry of the king of Ethiopia, an army beyond counting—and they (actually) had come to their assistance . . . I fought with them and inflicted a defeat upon them. In the melee of the battle, I personally captured alive the Egyptian charioteers with their princes and (also) the charioteers of the king of Ethiopia. . . . As to Hezekiah, the Jew, he did not submit to my yoke; I laid siege to 46 of his strong cities, walled forts and to the countless small villages in their vicinity, and conquered (them) by means of well-stamped (earth) ramps, and battering-rams brought (thus) near (to the walls) (combined with) the attack by foot soldiers (using) mines, breaches as well as sapper work. . . . Himself (Hezekiah) I made a prisoner in Jerusalem, his royal residence, like a bird in a cage. I surrounded him with earthwork in order to molest those who were leaving his city's gate. His towns which I had plundered I took away from his country and gave them (over) to Mitini, king of Ashdod, Padi, king of Ekron, and Sillibe, king of Gaza.

It is clear from this account that, for all his bluster and boasting, Sennacherib did not take Jerusalem, for reasons which we already know, from the Book of Isaiah, Chapter 37.

Then the angel of the Lord went forth, and smote the camp of the Assyrians a hundred and fourscore and five thousand; and when they arose early in the morning behold they were all dead corpses. So Sennacherib king of Assyria departed, and went and returned, and dwelt at Nineveh. And it came to pass, as he was worshipping at the house of Nisroch his god, that Adram-melech and Sharezer his sons smote him with the sword; and they escaped into the land of Armenia; and Esarhaddon his son reigned in his stead.

There is an interesting confirmation of this in another tablet found in the library of King Ashurbanipal, Sennacherib's grandson.

I tore out the tongues of those whose slanderous mouths had uttered blasphemies against my god Ashur and had plotted against me, his god-fearing prince; I defeated them (completely). The others, I smashed alive with the very same statues of protective deities with which they had smashed my own grandfather Sennacherib—now (finally) as a (belated) burial sacrifice for his soul. I fed their corpses, cut into small pieces to dogs, pigs . . . vultures, the birds of the sky and (also) to the fish of the ocean. After I had performed this and (thus) made quiet (again) the hearts of the great gods, my lords, I removed the corpses of those whom the pestilence had felled, whose leftovers (after) the dogs and pigs had fed on them were obstructing the streets, filling the places (of Babylon) (and of) those who had lost their lives through the terrible famine.[1]

[1] *Ancient Near Eastern Texts,* op. cit., p. 288. Princeton University Press, 1950.

This grim and horrible record, though it differs in some
details from that given in the Bible, confirms that the
Assyrian army was partly destroyed by a pestilence, and that
the survivors probably brought the plague to Nineveh on
their return.

Another fascinating aspect of these newly-discovered
Assyrian records was the way they linked up with the known
records of Ancient Egypt. For instance, Ashurbanipal, describing his campaigns against Egypt, says:

> Quickly I advanced as far as Kar-Baniti to bring speedy
> relief to the kings and regents in Egypt, servants who be-
> long to me. Tirkakah, king of Egypt and Nubia, heard in
> Memphis of the coming of my expedition and he called
> up his warriors for a decisive battle against me. Upon a
> trust (-inspiring) oracle (given) by Ashur, Bel, Nebo, the
> great gods, my lords, who (always) march at my side, I
> defeated the battle-(experienced) soldiers of his army in
> a great open battle. Tirkakah heard in Memphis of the
> defeat of his army (and) the (terror-inspiring) splendour
> of Ashur and Ishtar blinded him (thus) that he became a
> madman. . . .

Later the Assyrian regents rebel, and try to establish peace
with Tirkakah. They write to him, saying, "Let there be
peace between us and let us come to mutual understanding;
we will divide the country between us and no foreigner shall
rule over us." They scheme against the Assyrian army, but
the plot is detected and, in the words of Ashurbanipal:

> ". . . my officers heard about these matters, seized their
> mounted messengers with their messages, and (thus)
> learned about their rebellious doings. They arrested these
> kings and put their hands and feet in iron cuffs. . . . And
> they (the officers) put to the sword the inhabitants of the
> towns of Sais, Pindihi, Tanis and of all the other towns
> which had associated with them. They hung their corpses
> from stakes, flayed their skins and covered (with them)

the walls of the towns. Those kings who had repeatedly schemed, they brought alive to me to Nineveh. From all of them I had only mercy on Necho and granted him life. I made (a treaty) with him (protected by) oaths which greatly surpassed (those of the former treaty). I clad him in a garment with multicoloured trimmings, placed a golden chain on him (as the) insignia of his kingship, put golden rings on his hands; I wrote my name (phonetically) on an iron dagger (to be worn in) the girdle, the mounting of which was golden, and gave it to him. . . ."[1]

All these names are known from existing Egyptian records. Tirkakah (Taharka) was a Nubian (Sudanese) monarch who had marched up the Nile and conquered Egypt. His name is known from the temple records of Egypt, and he appears on the "king-lists". So does Necho, the Pharaoh whom Ashurbanipal befriended. And both Sais and Tanis are known to have been the royal residences of the Pharaohs when they ruled from the Delta. This astonishing correlation between Assyrian, Biblical and Egyptian records stirred the imaginations of scholars, Christian theologians and the educated public of Europe. It was this more than anything else which encouraged the Museums, learned societies and Governments of Britain, Germany, France and America to subscribe funds to further archaeological work in Mesopotamia. Disinterested scholarship played a part, yet I think it is true to say that the main impulse came from pious enthusiasts searching for a confirmation of Biblical truth. Unknowingly they were leading the way to discoveries of civilisations as far removed from Sennacherib as he was from the England of Victoria and the France of Napoleon III. The scholars whom they sponsored were to find writings in cuneiform written in the yet undeciphered Sumerian language which, though far older than the Bible, contained stories bearing a close resemblance to some of those in the Book of Genesis.

[1] *Ancient Near Eastern Texts*, op. cit., pp. 294–295. Princeton University Press, 1950.

But it is time to return to the nineteenth-century explorers, of whom one of the greatest was Sir Henry Layard, born in 1817, of British Huguenot stock. His parents divided their time between England, France, Switzerland and Italy, and Henry grew up with an appreciation of art and architecture which is uncommon among members of the British upper-middle-class. He had read with enthusiasm Rich's memoirs of Babylon and other Mesopotamian sites, and determined, when still a youth, to visit Iraq. The opportunity came when his parents sent him to Ceylon, hoping to interest him in tea-planting. His friends naturally assumed he would go by sea, but this was too slow for Henry. He elected to go via the more adventurous overland route with his young friend Mitford. They rode through Central Europe to Dalmatia, Montenegro, Albania and Bulgaria to Constantinople. Once there, Layard decided to go on to Petra "the rose-red city, half as old as time". Leaving Mitford behind, he rode on through Jerusalem, and Amman (where he was twice robbed) and so to Damascus, where he arrived, in the pouring rain, penniless, half-naked, on foot, to the embarrassment of the British Consul. Meanwhile the long-suffering Mitford fumed in Aleppo, where he was at length joined by the excited Layard, who had contrived to see Baalbeck and Beirut on the way. After a few days "to give my mare a rest" (Layard) the two travelled on through Urfah and Bisbks, arriving on the 2nd May at Mosul. Layard fell in love with Iraq, as have so many sensitive travellers.

> . . . desolation meets desolation [he wrote]. A feeling of awe succeeds to wonder; for there is nothing to relieve the mind, to lead to hope or to tell what has gone by. . . . These huge mounds of Assyria made a deeper impression on me, gave rise to more serious thoughts and reflections, than the temples of Baalbeck and the theatres of Ionia. . . .

Layard never reached Ceylon. He won the friendship of the British Resident in Baghdad, Colonel Taylor, a distinguished Orientalist; he studied the cuneiform inscriptions on the Behistun Rock, he browsed in Taylor's splendid library at Baghdad, and visited Khorsobad near Mosul, where Paul Emile Botta showed him his excavations in the fabulous capital of King Sargon II (eighth century B.C.) Here Botta had discovered a cuneiform inscription on which Rawlinson had identified the name of that king. For by this time (1843) the cuneiform was beginning to be read, and a wonderful new world was opening to archaeologists. The dreaded Assyrians, who, up to that time, had only been names in the Bible, were now revealed as real people; their splendid, powerful sculptures, in which their Kings were shown triumphing over their fallen enemies, were there for all Europe to see. Their impact on Europe was tremendous. Botta wrote to Paris:

> I believe myself to be the first who has discovered sculptures which with some reason can be referred to the period when Nineveh was flourishing.

Between 1843 and 1845 Layard contrived to get himself appointed to a diplomatic position on the staff of the British Ambassador to Turkey, Sir Stratford Canning. These were the days when "national prestige" was deeply involved with archaeological discoveries. Botta, a naturalist, who held the post of French Consular Agent in Baghdad, had stolen a march on the British. The French Government had liberally supported his excavations, and his "finds" were proudly exhibited in the Louvre. More and more magnificent examples of Assyrian sculpture were being shipped back to France in warships provided by the French Government. Reluctantly, the British authorities decided to do something about it. In 1844 Canning persuaded a reluctant British Museum to finance an excavation at Nimrud, conducted by his enthusiastic assistant, Henry Layard. As soon as this was agreed, Henry, in his own words:

> crossed the mountains of Pontus and the great steppes of the Usum Yilak as fast as post-horses could carry me, descended the high lands of the valley of the Tigris,

galloped over the vast plains of Assyria, and reached
Mosul in twelve days.

From 1846 to 1849, at Nimrud and Nineveh, he made discoveries as sensational as those of Botta at Khorsobad.

* * *

The discovery of the Assyrian palaces by Botta, Layard and
Rassam have no immediate bearing on the much older
civilisation of Sumer. Their importance lies in the fact that
the thousands of cuneiform tablets discovered by Layard in
Sennacherib's palace at Nineveh (1849) and by Rassam in his
excavation of the Palace of Ashurbanipal (1852) drew the
attention of philologists to a hitherto unknown literature of
great age. Though it employed the cuneiform system of
writing it was written in an *unknown language*. Fortunately
duplicate inscriptions were found written in a known tongue
—so that the mysterious writings could be read. We know
now that some of the folk-myths, epic poetry and legend
found in the Assyrian King's palace was as remote from
Sennacherib as he is from us. The Assyrian scribes had merely
copied and adapted them from earlier manuscripts. Layard
and his fellow-explorers, though unaware of this, had in
fact set the feet of later generations of scholars on the path
which led them to the discovery of a much earlier civilisation.

Among the tablets which Layard found in the library of
Ashurbanipal was a poem called "*Sa nagba imurur*" or "He
who saw everything". It is known now as *The Epic of Gilgamesh*. Gilgamesh was a folk-hero like Hercules, a god-like
man of prodigious strength, determination and courage.
Doughty fighter, persuasive and effectual lover, handsome,
shrewd and intelligent, Gilgamesh epitomises everything
which most men would like to be. He is so strong that the
God of the Forests gives way before him, so attractive to
women that even the Goddess of Love is enamoured by him,
so intelligent that he can pursue an idea to the ends of the
earth and persuade Utnapishtim—the only man who sur-

vived the Flood—to explain exactly how he won God's help and survived His vengeance on mankind.

Bewildered, fascinated, men who had been brought up on Holy Writ read the story of this mythical hero—transcribed from tablets of baked clay—which Layard and Rassum had found in the ruined galleries of Ashurbanipal's palace. They read the lines:

> *Man of Shuruppak, son of Ubar-Tutu*
> *Tear down (this) house, build a ship!*
> *Give up possessions, and seek thou life!*
> *Despise property and keep the soul alive!*
> *Aboard the ship take thou the seed of living things.*
> *The ship that thou shalt build*
> *Her dimensions shall be to measure.*
> *Equal shall be her width and her length.*
> *Like the Apsu shalt thou seal her. . . .*

And later in the story:

> *Consternation over Adad reaches the heavens,*
> *Turning to blackness all that has been light.*
> *(The wide) land is shattered like (a pot)*
> *For one day the south-storm (blew)*
> *Gathering speed as it blew (submerging the mountains)*
> *Overtaking the people like a battle.*
> *No one sees his fellow,*
> *Nor can people be recognised from heaven. . . .*

Had not they read this before somewhere, in the Book of Genesis?

And it came to pass after seven days that the waters of the Flood were upon the earth. . . . And the flood was forty days on the earth; and the waters increased, and bear up the Ark, and it was lift above the earth. . . . And the waters prevailed, were increased greatly upon the earth, and the Ark went upon the face of the waters. . . .

Later in *The Epic of Gilgamesh* occur these astonishing words.

> *. . . On Mount Nisir the ship came to a halt,*
> *Mount Nisir held the ship fast,*
> *Allowing no motion. . . .*
> *When the seventh day arrived,*
> *I sent forth and set free a dove.*
> *The dove came forth, but came back;*
> *There was no resting-place for her and she turned round.*
> *Then I sent forth and set free a swallow.*
> *The swallow went forth, but came back;*
> *There was no resting place for it and she turned round. . . .*

And so on, until eventually "a raven went forth, and seeing the waters had diminished, he eats, circles, caws, and turns not round".

It is virtually the Biblical story of Noah and the Ark. Yet, although the Palace of Ashurbanipal was of relatively late date—within seven hundred years of the birth of Christ—the original text was not in Hebrew. Nor was it in Assyrian, it was written in cuneiform—in an unknown language which probably belonged to a people who lived thousands of years before the warlike Assyrians conquered Mesopotamia. Probably because of its poetic or religious significance it had been translated into Assyrian just as the Greek poems of Homer were translated by the Romans, more than seven hundred years after they were written. But where had such literature been born? Certainly not in northern Assyria, for the topography was wrong. The description of the landscape with its wide-spreading plains, rainstorms and floods, hardly applied to northern Mesopotamia, where the rivers flow between rocky hills.

Looking further, linguists found an extraordinary story about Inanna, goddess of Love. She had dared to penetrate the underworld, the abode of the dead. First, however, she had prepared her elaborate toilet:

> *The sugurra, the crown of the plain, she has*
> *put upon her head,*
> *The wig of her forehead she has taken,*

The measuring rod (and) line of lapis lazuli
she has gripped in her hand,
Small lapis stones she has fastened about her neck,
Sparkling stones she has fastened to her breast,
A gold ring she has (about) her hand,
A breastplate (which) . . . she has tightened about
her breast,
Kohl (which) . . . she has daubed her eyes
With the pala-garment, the garment of ladyship,
she has covered her body. . . .

Boldly, if fearfully, Inanna enters the successive chambers of the Underworld, at the entrance to each of which she has to remove one of her garments, until at last she stands naked before the Queen of the Dead, who mocks her. Meanwhile, Earth, deprived of the presence of the Love-Goddess, languishes; the crops will not grow, nor the animals bear young. So, eventually, Inanna is released and makes her way slowly back to the sunlight. Then all is well again.

Is not this story also familiar in the much later Greek legend of Persephone, who was forced to spend a certain period of each year in the realms of Hephaestos, Lord of the Underworld? What was it doing in the archives of an Assyrian warrior-king in the eighth century B.C.?

But echoes of pagan mythology had far less impact on Europeans of the nineteenth century than the stories which though not Scriptural, bore a close relationship to the Holy Scripture. And as, gradually, the little baked-clay tablets and cylinders began to yield their secrets, the learned world became less and less interested in large, impressive stone monuments, which could be unearthed and transported to Europe; they wanted no longer merely to see and wonder; they wanted to *know*.

Once their novelty had died the sculptured reliefs from the palaces of Ezarhaddon, Sennacherib and Ashurbanipal, even though they brought to life the dreaded Assyrians of the Old Testament, made less impact. After all, the Assyrians and

Babylonians came relatively late in Biblical history, between 800 and 600 B.C. True, they were mentioned in the Bible, but so were other unknown cities and peoples which may have existed long before the Assyrian and Babylonian empires. Where, for instance, was *Calneh* and *Erech* and *Ur of the Chaldees*? The technique of comparative dating by pottery had not yet been developed, yet already light was beginning to glow in the darker reaches of the time-tunnel. Nimrud, Nineveh and even Babylon were clearly not the beginning. There must have been other, older peoples further back in time.

Men turned again to the Old Testament, puzzling over that splendid passage in the Book of Genesis which begins:

And the whole earth was of one language, and of one speech. And it came to pass, as they journeyed from the east, that they found a plain in the land of Shinar; and they dwelt there. And they said to one another, "Go to, let us make bricks, and burn them thoroughly." And they had brick for stone, and slime[1] for mortar. And they said "Go on, let us build a city and a tower, whose top may reach heaven; and let us make us a name, lest we be scattered abroad upon the face of the earth."

[1] Nowadays translated as *bitumen*, which is abundant in Iraq.

CHAPTER FOUR

THE DISCOVERY OF ERECH

In a book as brief as this one, some telescoping is inevitable, and while the story so far revealed is true in broad outline, it would be misleading to suggest that the discovery of Sumer followed automatically the uncovering of the Assyrian cities and the decipherment of the cuneiform writing. Oscar Wilde's epigram—"the truth is seldom pure and never simple"—is as true of archaeology as it is in a more general context.

For instance, scholars were already thinking and speculating about the "land of Shinar" long before the tablets found in the libraries of Ashurbanipal and Sennacherib could be fully understood. An Englishman named William Kennett Loftus, who travelled extensively in Mesopotamia between 1849 and 1852, wrote a book of which one chapter begins thus:

> The position of this land of Shinar is a much disputed point, and grave discussion has arisen concerning its identification. Some writers, from similarity of name, contend that it refers to the modern district called Sinjar, in Mesopotamia, between Mosul on the Tigris and Bir on the Euphrates; but the coincidence goes no further, for Shinar is described in the Bible as "a plain" whereas Sinjar is an undulating, rocky region traversed by lofty limestone mountains. Others [he continued] . . . point to a district

47

much further to the south, where are the remains of innumerable ancient cities, regarded by Jewish tradition as
the country of Shinar, from whence that nation originally
proceeded. In confirmation of this, Babylonia, in the old
cuneiform inscriptions, is called by the same name—
Shinar, and it is likewise still preserved in the important
ruins of Sinkara. The site of Babel is, moreover, tradi-
tionally assigned to the same region, and the large ruins
near Hillah on the Euphrates are generally supposed to
represent it.[1]

Reading this staid, pedantic prose one might imagine an
elderly Victorian scholar theorising from the depths of his
study chair. In fact Loftus was an ardent and adventurous
young man who, between 1849 and 1852, undertook long
dangerous journeys on horseback through the wildest part of
unexplored Mesopotamia. His feeling for landscape has
already been mentioned in an earlier passage from his
fascinating book *Travels and Researches in Chaldea and Susiana*;
here, as a contrast, is an example of his sense of humour, and
his exasperated affection for the wild tribesmen who inhabited the ancient lands he was endeavouring to study. At
Warka he tried vainly with his Arab helpers to obtain intact
specimens of a certain type of baked-clay coffin.

They invariably fell to pieces in the attempt to stir them.
Sometimes the contents were removed, and at other times
the earth, which had accumulated inside the crevices, was
wholly allowed to remain, or was partially cleared out;
pieces of carpet and abbas were tied around, and poles
placed below them to give support, but all to no purpose.
After several days of anxious labour and the demolition of
perhaps a hundred coffins, I almost despaired of success.
The Arabs were anxious that I should be pleased, and
were as annoyed as myself at our fruitless endeavours. At
last the good-natured Gunza took hold of my sleeve, and
addressed me on behalf of his fellows:

[1] Loftus, W. K., op. cit.

Oh, Beg! you take much trouble to get one of these pots of the old *Kaffirs*—may they be cursed!—and have brought with you spades and shovels from a great distance for this purpose. Our hands were not made to use such implements, which are the tools of the *Fellah* (peasants); but with the spear we can do many things. Give us your permission, Beg, and we will follow our own mode of search, and, *inshallah*! we shall soon be able to find plenty of pots, among which there will certainly be one strong and good enough to carry away."

Gunza was right. His tribe, the *Tuweyba*, were warriors more accustomed to handling the spear than the spade. But they were extremely skilful tomb-robbers. Before very long several intact "pots" i.e. pottery coffins, were found. Loftus had them strengthened with layers of paper, ready for transport to the river and thence to far-off England. Then the trouble started. Loftus continues:

The ground was, in many parts, excessively rough and difficult to traverse . . . so that I was in constant trepidation lest a trip or false step might destroy the fruits of our labour. This anxiety on our part was not without cause, for the wild fellows, notwithstanding the weight of their burden, could not be restrained from joining in dance and song, with which their comrades duly enlivened the whole route. Their excitement had been roused to the highest pitch, and their gestures surpassed anything they had ever exhibited before me. The coffin was frequently in danger when the whole party sometimes feigned a hostile charge against the bearers, and the latter, unable to restrain their natural impetuosity, wielded their spears, which they insisted on carrying, and yelled defiance in return. The more entreated, the more riotous they became, until I discovered that the best plan was to let them have their own way and wear themselves out.

When the procession of men carrying the coffins arrived at the river the excitement reached its peak.

The women, in their eagerness to see the unwonted sight—
unwonted indeed, because probably upwards of two thousand years had passed since such a coffin had been con-
veyed in a similar manner—even forgot to hide their
faces, and came out in a body to meet the procession,
uttering their wild *tahlehl* and plaintive wail, while they
pretended to throw dust on their hair, in imitation of the
ceremony of mourning the dead.[1] The men, under the influence of this additional impulse, redoubled their exer-
tions, until they resembled frantic demons rather than
human beings. I was not sorry when the primitive bier and
its precious burden were safely deposited in our tents.

Loftus, a geologist, first visited Mesopotamia as a member
of the Turco-Persian Frontier Commission of 1849–52. For
many centuries the long frontier between Turkey and Persia
had been in a highly unsettled state. There was both religious
and political animosity, and when, in 1839–40 serious hosti-
lities between the two countries appeared imminent, the
Governments of Great Britain and Russia offered 'Friendly
mediation'. After a meeting of delegates at Ezereum, a
treaty was concluded, one article of which determined that
'representatives should be sent to survey and define a precise
line of boundary which will not admit of further dispute'.
Had it not been for this political crisis, Loftus and his friends
would have had no reason for visiting such a dangerous
and inhospitable land and the rediscovery of Sumer would
probably have occurred later, and in a different manner.

The first part of the journey seems to have been highly en-
joyable, and Loftus paints a delightful picture of the British
and Tsarist officials and their staffs floating down the
Euphrates on a *kelek*.

It was midspring. Instead of the arid sands, which the
word "desert" implies to the uninitiated in Mesopotamian

---

[1] An exactly similar scene took place in Egypt in 1881, when the rediscovered bodies of the Pharaohs were removed from their resting-place
near Luxor and taken by steamer to Cairo. L.C.

travel, broad plains of the richest verdure, enlivened with flowers of every hue, met our delighted gaze on either side of the noble river. Coleopterous insects swarmed upon the banks, culling the sweets of the fleeting vegetation. The cry of the velvet-breasted francolin, and the sand-grouse rushing overhead like an irresistible wind, enticed the most ardent of our party to land, and indulge the love of their favourite sport. . . . Now and then a herd of wild boars was discovered among the jungle, or observed crossing the river. . . . A bend of the stream sometimes brought us suddenly upon a large Bedouin encampment, whence, on observing the raft, a score or so of swarthy Arab dames, with piercing black eyes and never-failing rows of the whitest teeth, launched forth in inflated sheep skins, and paddled out to meet the *"keleks"*. . . . Never did a merrier party than ours float down the Tigris upon a fragile raft.

They visited the usual places; Babylon, Birs Nimrud, The Tomb of Ezekiel, Kerbella, Baghdad (where they spent Christmas) and then arranged that "the . . . armed steamer *Nitocris* under the command of Captain Felix Jones, . . . should convey the whole party to Mohammerah, the southern part of the disputed boundary line. The mules, horses and servants were to proceed by land".

Loftus elected to travel by the land route

influenced by a twofold object; that of examining the geology of the Chaldean marshes, and that of exploring the ruins of Warka, to which native tradition assigns the honour of being the birthplace of the patriarch Abraham. Colonel Williams (the head of the Mission) ever ready to afford facilities to scientific enterprises, not only granted a willing consent to my proposal to join the overland party, but also suggested that Mr. Churchill should accompany me.

Harry Churchill was also young and adventurous, and one can see readily why Loftus preferred to take the tough

overland route with a congenial companion rather than accompany the main body of the Commission on its stately progress down the Euphrates. His imagination had been stirred
by the antiquities he had already seen—Nineveh, Nimrud,
Babylon; but he was even more excited by reports he had
heard of other ancient cities in the relatively unknown land
to the south. "Examining the geology of the Chaldean
marshes," one suspects, was merely an alibi. It was not geology which interested William Loftus at that moment, but
archaeology—that, and the prospect of meeting new
people; wild tribes such as the *Tuweyba*, the Apej and the
Zobaial Arabs.

I make no apology for quoting at length from Loftus's
narrative, because, unlike the modern archaeologist describing well-trodden territory, this young Victorian traveller
approaches Shinar with all the wonder and enthusiasm of a
young man aware that he is seeing an ancient land *for the
first time*. From Babylon he struck eastwards across the desert
towards the ruins of Niffar, a journey of two days—

across a level and sandy desert, intersected by an infinity of
ancient water-courses, whose streams had for centuries
back ceased to flow, their very existence being sometimes
only faintly indicated by the darker colour of the soil,
arising from the salts contained in it. Now and then a low
mound of a few fragments of pottery, bricks and glass,
assisted us to beguile the time by speculations and discussions on the former inhabitants of the land, and in
making comparisons between past and present. . . . In this
manner, and in taking careful notes and observations of the
route, the hours passed rapidly, and we fully enjoyed the
novelty of the scene before us in that deserted and barren
plain—for so it may be called, because the inhabited and
cultivated spots are few and far between, in comparison
with the wide expanse of rich land uninhabited and uncultivated throughout Mesoptamia. Independently, however, of the strange associations called forth by bricks and

pottery, the journey was delightful, from the excitement of knowing that an unexplored region lay before us. . . .

On every side, as the two companions rode on across the arid plain of southern Iraq, they found remains of great canals and tributary watercourses which had once carried the waters of the Twin Rivers far inland, watering what were once fields and orchards; a complex system of irrigation which could only have been devised by a highly civilised people. Millions must once have lived on this land which was now utterly barren and deserted, save for the occasional cluster of black Bedouin tents. Sometimes the travellers came upon great mounds of crumbling mud-brick, all that were left of large cities, dominated by a ruined *ziggurat* or tiered tower such as they had already seen at Nimrud and Babylon. Millions of potsherds testified to long period of occupation. Sometimes they found vast cemeteries in which the Arabs poked and prodded among the bones of the dead, looking for gold beads and other ornaments which they could sell.

The whole region of Lower Chaldaea abounds in sepulchral cities of immense extent. . . . It is difficult to convey anything like the correct notion of the piles upon piles of human relics which there utterly astound the beholder. Except only the triangular space between the three principal ruins (of Warka) the whole remainder of the platform, the whole space between the walls, and an unknown extent of desert beyond them, are everywhere filled with the bones and sepulchres of the dead.

Yet, vast and lonely though the landscape was, the travellers could not escape the attentions of the few indigenous inhabitants, Arab tribesmen whose goodwill it was necessary to secure, and who sometimes asked pertinent questions. Loftus records the following conversation with Sheikh Fahad (The Tiger), head of the Muntefik tribe:

Loftus. Do many Europeans pass through Sukesh-Sheioukh?

Fahad. No! what should induce them to come so far from their own homes in Firengistan?

Loftus. The Arab loves the shade of his own tent, and the Firenghi (European) is equally attached to the land of his birth, but the latter travels into far distant countries, to see the world, gain instruction, and impart it to his friends on his return. Some travel on business—others for pleasure. Many, like myself, are partial to visiting old ruins, like Babel, Niffar and Warka. The Arabs think us mad for our pains.

Fahad. Perhaps so. What is the use of your seeing them?

Loftus. They afford us many relics—such as writing on bricks—which throw light on the past not otherwise obtainable. From them we learn that *our* forefathers were *yours* also!

"He seemed," adds Loftus, "to doubt this fact, for how could a Ghyawr be related to a good Mussulman?"

So they travelled on, until they reached the wide-spreading marshes at the head of the Persian Gulf, where, at flood-time, the tops of the palm trees are just visible above the green water, over which clouds of bright-plumaged birds swoop and hover in the humid air. This was the land of the Deluge, the legendary site of the Garden of Eden, where today air travellers night-stopping at Basra lie panting in their hotel rooms, kept awake by the eerie croaking of innumerable frogs.

*   *   *

When after many weeks they returned to make their report to Colonel Williams, they overwhelmed him with wonderful stories of a vanished civilisation, evidences of a former dense population, and the huge massive piles, covered with fragments of stone and pottery, which loom up from the plains and marshes of ancient Chaldaea. Such names as Nuffar, Hammam, Tel Jide, Warka, Muquayyar, formerly seen by only two other Europeans[1] aroused intense interest, for now

[1] G. Baillie Fraser and Dr. Ross in 1834.

that the cuneiform writing was beginning to be read, there was the possibility that inscriptions might be found which would reveal the names of long-dead cities. Williams agreed that Loftus should return to one of the mounds he had discovered, at Warka, and with the help of two friends, Kerr Lynch and Boucher, make trial excavations.

The work was terribly arduous. Sometimes sandstorms arose, and "a dense cloud of impalpable sand" drove the workmen from their places, so that they often lost their way in returning to camp.

At sunrise [Loftus wrote] I set out with the Arabs for the mounds ... and never left them during the whole day. The soil was so light that, in walking from trench to trench, my feet were buried at each step. ... It was usually long after sunset ere we returned to camp, stumbling every instant over the broken ground. A few minutes sufficed me to swallow the food my cook had prepared when almost tired to death, I was obliged to lay down plans from my rough notes, write my journal, and pack the objects procured in the course of the day. On many occasions it was two o'clock in the morning before I retired to rest, perfectly benumbed from the intensity of the cold, which even the double walls of my little tent could not exclude.

But the ruins of the unknown city which the Arabs called Warka were too enormous for the resources of Loftus's little party. For three months they slaved at the mounds, which formed "an irregular circle, nearly six miles in circumference, defined by traces of an earthen rampart, in some parts fifty feet high". They explored a pyramidal hill, a hundred feet high, called Buweriye ("reed matting") which represented a stage tower or *ziggurat*. They found and partly unearthed a remarkable complex of public buildings consisting of a large outer court flanked by a number of halls and smaller rooms. They found part of a wall, thirty feet long, entirely composed of small cones of terracotta, three and a half inches long. "Some had been dipped in red and black colour and were arranged in various ornamental patterns, such as diamonds, triangles, zigzags and stripes." This form of decoration, until then unknown, we now recognise as typical of Sumerian architecture.

But at the end Loftus and his companions had to return to Baghdad with little to show save a few small portable antiquities,

> less than a hundred so-called contract tablets of the Neo-Babylonian, Persian and even Seleucid dynasties ... an interesting small tablet in serpentine with pictures on the one side and four lines of early cuneiform characters on the other ... a brick with stamp in relief of an elevated altar surmounted by a seven-rayed sun; several terra-cotta figurines; a thin silver plate embossed with a beautiful female figure. ...

and so on.

But Loftus's superficial scratching had one result of outstanding importance. Among the inscriptions was one which Rawlinson was able to decipher as the name *Erech*. It was the ancient name of the city, the same name which occurs in the book of Genesis.

> And Cush begat Nimrud. And the beginning of his kingdom was Babel, and *Erech*, and Accad and Calneh in the land of Shinar ...

CHAPTER FIVE

REVELATION OF SUMER

AFTER the discovery of Erech other Sumerian sites were gradually revealed. Loftus dug at Senkara, finding tablets which enabled Rawlinson to identify the city as Larsa, the "Ellasar" of the Old Testament. J. E. Taylor, the British Vice-Consul at Basra, started to examine the huge mounds of Tell Muqquyar near Nasiryah. After driving tunnels into what appeared to be the ruins of a *ziggurat*, he unearthed at the foot of one corner a small inscribed cylinder. Similar cylinders were found at the other corners, evidently "foundation deposits" which the Sumerians, like other ancient peoples, buried under their temples. The moment when Rawlinson announced his decipherment was a dramatic one. For whereas such Biblical names as Erech and Ellasar did not immediately strike a chord, millions of Jews and Christians knew Ur of the Chaldees, the birthplace of Abraham, and it was this name—Ur—which Rawlinson read on the cylinder. Another Biblical city which for thousands of years had been only a name, could now be placed on the map. Later, in 1855, Taylor discovered and identified ancient Eridu.

Further impetus to the Sumeriology was given by a young Englishman named George Smith. Smith was no well-born gentleman adventurer such as Loftus or Layard. He was an engraver of bank-notes. As his place of work was near the British Museum, Smith used to spend his lunch-hours there, poring over the cuneiform documents which fascinated him, and which he was learning to decipher. A member of the Museum's staff, noting the young man's interest, encouraged him to further study, and eventually offered him a minor post in the Museum. Among Smith's first tasks was to sort out and classify the tablets which Layard had found in the palace of Ashurbanipal at Nineveh. This was how the historic "Flood" tablet was discovered, in Smith's own words:

> . . . I soon found half of a curious tablet which had evidently contained originally six columns. . . . On looking down the third column, my eye caught the statement that *the ship rested on the mountain of Nizir,* followed by an account of the sending forth of the dove . . . I saw at once that I had here discovered a portion at least of the Chaldaean account of the Deluge.

This discovery made such an impact, particularly in the Press, that the London *Daily Telegraph* arranged for Smith to go to Mesopotamia to find the other half of the tablet. The extraordinary fact is that, after cutting through the mounds of debris left by Layard and other explorers, Smith *did* find the tiny missing fragment.[1] Four years later he died of dysentery contracted in a journey across the desert from Mosul to the Mediterranean. He was the first Assyriologist to die in the service of archaeology.

The decipherment of the cuneiform also marks a change in the attitude of the learned world towards Mesopotamian excavation. In the days of Rich, Layard and Loftus, the digging of ancient sites was more like mining than archaeology. Understaffed and short of funds, excavators tunnelled desperately into the mounds, trying, in the short time available, to find portable antiquities which they could ship back to the European museums which had financed the excavations. The more they found the better was their chance of getting a new and larger grant for future work. In 1851, for instance, Leon Faucher, Minister of the Interior, persuaded the French National Assembly to vote 70,000 francs towards

[1] Quoted in Chapter 12, p. 128.

the organisation of "a scientific and artistic expedition to Mesopotamia and Media". The expedition was led by Fulgence Fresnel, formerly French consul at Jidda, assisted by Jules Oppert as Assyriologist and Felix Thomas as architect.

But their work at Babylon, where Oppert thought he had located the Hanging Gardens, was handicapped by similar misfortunes to those which had beset their predecessors; ill-health, inadequate resources, official obstruction, and the frustration of being able only to scratch the surface of the buried city. Though they worked for two years, at the end of that time Babylon was still virtually unexplored; and even the precious objects which the French expedition had uncovered—including the marble vase of King Naram-Sin—were lost when the barge carrying them foundered in the Euphrates. However, the expedition produced notable scientific results. Oppert's two volumes—*Expedition Scientifique en Mesopotamie*, published in Paris in 1856, are remarkable both for the archaeological information they contain and for the skill with which the author translates and interprets the cuneiform inscriptions.

But during the seventies and eighties a gradual change took place. Archaeologists were sent out on organized expeditions, financed by their Governments, by Universities or Museums, and encouraged to make a thorough, leisurely exploration of a few selected sites over a number of years; the emphasis now was less on finding loot for museums and galleries, and more on scientific information. There was also an increasing tendency to explore the unknown sites in southern Mesopotamia. Among the most successful of these expeditions was that led by Ernest de Sarzec, formerly French Vice-Consul at Basra, the first man to excavate thoroughly a large Sumerian city and reveal its fascinating art to the world. De Sarzec, incidentally, had at least one thing in common with Heinrich Schliemann, discoverer of Troy. Like that great German archaeologist, he took his young bride with him to share the honour—and the hardships—of his excavations.

The site he chose was Telloh, situated at the tail of the Shatt al Hai canal. De Sarzec did not himself discover Telloh, but heard about it from a certain Mr. J. Asfar, who had interests in a steamship company called the *Strick-Asfar*, and also dealt in antiquities. By this time the commercial value of these hitherto valueless objects was becoming known in the *souks* of Baghdad and Mosul, and thus a new element entered into Mesopotamian archaeology—rivalry between the officially sponsored archaeological expeditions working under permit, and the resourceful dealers in illicitly acquired objects. A similar situation had arisen in Egypt.

De Sarzec did not at first apply for a permit from the Turkish Government, for fear of arousing the interest of Hormudz Rassam, successor to Layard (who by this time had retired from archaeology to become Her Majesty's Minister Plenipotentiary at the Court of Madrid). Rassam stepped into his shoes, and, on behalf of the British Museum, "obtained a concession . . . which authorised him to excavate almost unconditionally on all Crown lands in the Pashaliks of Baghdad, Aleppo and Van in eastern Anatolia".[1]

Without informing the Turkish Government de Sarzec dug trial trenches into the mounds of Telloh from March to June 1877, and found a number of fine diorite statues (some of which had already been unearthed by Asfar) and a considerable amount of inscribed material. All these he took to Paris and sold to the Louvre for 130,000 francs. Meanwhile Rassam, the eager bloodhound of the British Museum, had picked up the scent, and himself applied to dig at Telloh. To his chagrin he discovered that his *firman*, though extensive in scope, did not permit him to excavate this particular site. De Sarzec, in the meanwhile, successfully applied for a permit, and was thus able to work at Telloh for many years, unhindered by Rassam's plundering gangs—for they were little better. Rassam still worked on the old system—sending groups of Arab labourers to peck away at sites here and there throughout Iraq, sometimes leaving them unsupervised for

[1] Lloyd, Seton. *Foundations in the Dust*, Oxford University Press, 1947.

months at a time. All they wanted was loot for the British Museum; this was not his fault, of course, but that of the system under which he worked. Other countries behaved just as badly in the cause of "national prestige".

It is difficult to exaggerate the impact which de Sarzec's Telloh sculptures made upon the intelligentsia of Paris in the last quarter of the nineteenth century. It was not merely antiquarians and Biblical scholars who were fascinated, but artists also. For some four hundred years European art had been dominated by the artists of the Renaissance, and, through them, by the Greek or Roman masters who they had rediscovered. There had been a "Greek Revival" and the Parthenon sculptures brought back to Europe by Lord Elgin had had a revivifying effect. Still, the experience of Greek art was not new and strange; it flowed into the main stream of European culture. In the early years of the nineteenth century Ancient Egyptian sculpture had made a temporary impression (mainly in the vulgar "Empire" furniture of the Napoleonic era) but its influence was superficial. The majestic severity of the Old Kingdom, and the fluid grace of the New Kingdom, had no perceptible effect on European art.

But with the art of ancient Sumer it was different. The great contemporary artists of the French School, whose genius was to mould the taste of future generations, were profoundly influenced. As Sir Leonard Woolley writes of Sumerian sculptures:

> The pleasure which they give is independent of any question of their age or school, of the sources from which they sprang, of the conditions which helped to shape them and of the traditions they embody.[1]

These objects, he says "make a direct appeal to our sense of beauty and can justly be treasured for their artistic merit".

All this is profoundly true, but in the present author's opinion, it is equally true of the art of Ancient Egypt. Why is it that Egyptian painting and sculpture, with its subtle

[1] Woolley, Sir L. *The Development of Sumerian Art*, Faber & Faber, 1935.

strength, vigour and sophistication, has had relatively little effect on modern European art, whereas the art of Sumer has? My own view is that the revelation of Ancient Egyptian art came *too soon*, before men had come to question the validity of the Graeco-Roman tradition. Sumerian art was rediscovered just at the time when sensitive Europeans had begun to question the classical view of life and were searching for a new approach to reality. They have moved much further since, finding inspiration in Polynesian idols and African ju-ju masks, but the breakaway from the classical tradition began when visitors crowded into the Louvre to gaze at the sculptured figures which de Sarzec had dug from the mounds of Telloh, over eighty years ago.

CHAPTER SIX

THE SECRET OF THE WRITINGS

ARMED with a special grant from the French Government, de Sarzec resumed his excavations at Telloh in 1880, and for two seasons systematically investigated the mounds, finding more and more splendid statues of the *patesi* (Governors) of Lagash (the ancient name of the city). These are now among the splendours of the Louvre, but one of them, found later, can be seen in the Babylonian Room of the British Museum. He also found the remains of a Sumerian temple, vases and bricks with the names of Ur-Nana, Entemmena and other Kings of Lagash, and the well-known Stele of Vultures, together with a number of baked-clay prisms inscribed with the history and exploits of the Governor Gudea, whose numerous portrait-statues have made him the most familiar of Sumerian rulers.

However, although de Sarzec worked at Lagash for many years, he was faced with an immense task. There were seventeen large mounds, and even in 1891, when Sir Wallis Budge visited the site, considerable areas had still to be explored. Moreover, as the years passed the French excavator spent less and less time at the site; meanwhile illicit diggers, employed by the dealers of Baghdad, tunnelled into the mounds in de Sarzec's absence, seeking the hoard of baked-clay tablets which most archaeologists believed must exist there. For it was apparent that Lagash had been not only the residence of a Prince, but also a thriving mercantile and commercial centre. Therefore, somewhere among the piles of rubbish there must exist the merchants' file of accounts and transactions such as had been found on other Mesopotamian sites.

At length [writes Budge] the unauthorized diggers found what they were looking for, a small compact mound, in which was a series of little chambers containing baked-clay inscribed tablets. The news of their discovery spread, as such things will, with extraordinary rapidity; but before they had made arrangements to remove the tablets and pull down the chambers, de Sarzec appeared at Al Basrah. The diggers hurriedly shovelled back the stones and earth over the chambers, and began to dig another mound, one which de Sarzec had partially excavated. When he came to Telloh he was greeted by cries of joy in the Arab fashion; but everyone denied all knowledge of any discovery of tablets. His former overseers went to work with him as before; but with one excuse and another they succeeded in keeping him from attempting to dig in the mound containing the tablets.[1]

Eventually, when de Sarzec had left, some 40,000 tablets were unearthed, varying in size from about 12 in. to 2½ in. square, and most of them in as perfect a state as when they were stored some 4,500 years ago. There were lists of grain and animals, inventories of sheep and cattle, lists of workmen employed by the temple (with their rations) and numerous contracts. A brisk trade then ensued, even the captains of the river-boats and office clerks buying and selling tablets for a quick profit. "Every buyer," writes Budge, "exported his purchases as quickly as possible; and so the great collection of Telloh tablets, at least 35,000 in number, were scattered all over the civilised world."[1]

Such was the atmosphere in which Mesopotamian archaeology was carried on seventy years ago; a confused mixture of international rivalry, personal jealousy and com-

[1] Budge, Sir E. Wallis. *Rise and Progress of Assyriology*, M. Hopkinson & Co., 1925.

mercial cupidity; yet, running through all this, was a pure thread of honest, devoted scientific research by men of many nations, British, French, German, American, Italian, Swiss and Scandinavian. Some of these scholars went to Mesopotamia and dug. A greater number, the philologists, worked on the further decipherment of the cuneiform writing, of which more and more examples were found and published. In Britain there were scholars such as Gadd, Hincks, Knudtzon, Campbell Thompson, Smith, Sayce and Johns; in France, besides Botta, Oppert and de Sarzec, whom we have already met, such men as Dieulafoy, Longperrier, Menant and Lenormant carried on the tradition. In Switzerland Julius Weber and Etienne Combe, in Italy Philoxene Luzzato and Bruto Teloni, in Scandinavia Knut Leonard Tallquist and in Holland Cnoop Koopmans, all added to the corpus of knowledge. But perhaps the greatest strides were made in the universities of Germany.

We have seen how a German scholar, Grotefend, was the first man to break the secret of the cuneiform, but though he continued to publish papers until 1856, some German Orientalists began to doubt the accuracy of some of his translations. Among these was Eberhard Schrader (1836–1908) "the Father of Assyriology" in Germany. Schrader made a careful study of Rawlinson's works, and finally accepted his system. He published, among other works, a transcription of the trilingual inscription of Darius I on the Behistun Rock, a translation of the Assyrian text of the "Descent of Ishtar into the Underworld", and his great work *Keilinschriften und das Alte Testament* (1883) established his reputation in the world of international scholarship. "He was", says Budge, "a fine example of the old type of German scholar; his modesty was as great as his learning." A younger scholar, Friedrich Delitsch (1850–1923) formed a class for students of Assyrian and prepared a Reading Book (*Assyrische Lesetücke*) with a Grammar and Syllabary. His personal influence among German students was great, as was that of his pupil Carl Bezold (1859–1922). Bezold was a familiar figure in London, which he visited frequently to study Assyrian texts in the British Museum. His greatest ambition was to publish a great Assyrian Dictionary, but death overtook him before he could complete the work.

Mighty battles were fought in this obscure field of learning. For instance a French Orientalist named Halevy denied, for a time, that a Sumerian Language existed. In many historical inscriptions found on Mesopotamian sites there occur the words "King of Sumer and Akkad". Akkad, we now know, was the northern part of ancient Sumer, occupied by a Semitic race—the Akkadians—who, though racially distinct from the Sumerians, shared similar religious beliefs (e.g. the Sumerian gods have Akkadian features). Halevy was obsessed by a belief that all the great cultures of Western Asia had a Semitic origin. He suggested that the earliest dwellers in southern Mesopotamia were Semitic Akkadians and that their language was "Akkadian". He believed that the so-called "Sumerian" language was in fact a secret form of writing invented by the Semitic Babylonian priests, and not a separate tongue. Oppert, on the other hand, firmly maintained that it was a distinct language of its own—the tongue of the earliest inhabitants of Babylonia whom he called "Sumerian". For a long time Halevy's mistaken views were widely accepted even by Delitsch. But in the end it was proved by Sayce, Lenorment, Hommel and others that the former views of Rawlinson were correct. The Sumerians were a separate people. An Englishman, Professor Landon, published the first Sumerian Grammar in 1914.

Other German scholars followed Schrader, Delitsch and Bezold; Ludwig Abel who assisted Winckler in his publication of the famous Amarna Letters, Walter Andraw, Rudolph Brunow, Erich Ebling and Friedrich Hrozny (better known perhaps for his work on the Hittite cuneiform tablets found in Asia Minor); Peter Jensen published among other works, *Das Gilgamesh-Epos in der Weltliteratur* and *Die Kosmologie de Babylonier*, and Bruno Meissner produced a useful digest of facts concerning the civilisation of Sumer,

Babylon and Assyria—a work of the same class as Wilkinson's useful work on Egypt *Manners and Customs of the Ancient Egyptians*.

I offer no apology for this long—and perhaps to some tedious—list of great names. For these distinguished scholars, few of whom enjoyed the excitement of digging in the mounds of Babylonia, did as much or perhaps even more than the excavators to reveal the civilisation of ancient Sumer. In some ways we owe more to them than to the Egyptologists. For whereas in Egypt there was one people, one language, one culture, in Mesopotamia there were several peoples, languages, cultures. There were the Assyrians, who came late, there were the Sargonid Babylonians who preceded them, and still further back in time were the mysterious Sumerians and Akkadians whose culture, religion and writing-system had been partly adopted by the later inhabitants of Mesopotamia.

Moreover, while all these peoples—and others such as the Persians and the Hittites—used the same system of writing, many separate languages were involved. To use a homely though inexact parallel it was as if, four thousand years hence, future archaeologists discovered documents written in English, French, German, Italian, Dutch, Norwegian and Latin—*yet all using the same Latin alphabet.* Faced with such a confusing mass of evidence, and with little corroborative detail to help him save the crumbling remains of long-dead cities, how would our archaeologist of A.D. 6000 establish that the Roman civilisation came first and that documents in the European languages might have been written at any time between 500 and 1,500 years later?

CHAPTER SEVEN

THE CONTINUING SEARCH

The Sumeriologist [writes Professor S. N. Kramer] is one of the narrowest of specialists in the highly-specialised academic halls of learning, a well-nigh perfect example of the man who "knows most about the least". He cuts his world down to that small part of it known as the Middle East. . . . He confines his researches to the written documents discovered in Mesopotamia, primarily clay tablets inscribed in the cuneiform script, and restricts his contributions to texts written in the Sumerian language. . . . Incredible as it may seem, however, this pinpoint historian, this Toynbee in reverse, has something of unusual interest to offer to the general reader. The Sumeriologist, more than most other scholars and specialists, is in a position to satisfy man's universal quest for origins—for "firsts" in the history of civilisation.[1]

In the preceding chapters I have tried to show how our knowledge of Sumer has gradually been filtered out of masses of archaeological data left by the various occupants of ancient Mesopotamia. This data takes many forms; ruined cities containing the superincumbent layers of some four millenia; temples, palaces, dwellings, pottery, grave-furniture, domestic and religious objects, and innumerable documents written in several languages. The "filter" simile is a

[1] Kramer, S. N. *From the Tablets of Sumer*, Falcon's Wing Press, Indian Hills, Colorado, U.S.A.

reasonably precise one; like the botanist fishing specimens
from a pond, the archaeologist may find on one site neo-
Babylonian remains dating from the time of Nebuchadnezzar
(605–562 B.C.) of the Assyrian king Shalmaneser I (*c.* 1276
B.C.) of the Babylonian king Khammurabi (*c.* 2130–2087
B.C.) of Sargon (2750 B.C.) and, right at the bottom, objects
left by the Sumerians who ruled from Ur, or Lagash, or
Eridu in about 3000 B.C. (And even these would not be the
earliest remains.) The documents found in these various
layers might range from Persian (*c.* 500 B.C.) to Sumerian
(*c.* 3000 B.C.). The period they cover is greater than that
which stretches between the time of Pericles and that of
Harold Wilson. Yet all use the same cuneiform writing-
system.

From about 1880 onwards the various deposits were
gradually filtered out; Assyriologists tended to concentrate
more and more on the archaeology of their own selected
period; so did the students of Babylonia; gradually these elements were filtered off, and there remained the sediment of
ancient Sumer, about which hardly anything had been
known save the obscure references in the Book of Genesis, and
the Sumerian writings which the Babylonians and Assyrians
had translated and preserved. Until these were found and
identified as Sumerian, there was, as Professor Kramer observes—

> no recognizable trace either of the land or of its people in
> the entire literature available to the modern scholar. The
> very name Sumer had been erased from the mind and the
> memory of man for more than two thousand years. . . .
> Yet today the Sumerians are one of the best-known peoples
> of the ancient Near East.[1]

How has this come about? Mainly because after de Sarzec's excavations at Telloh had confirmed the existence of a
Sumerian people, a separate branch of archaeology was
established. Within this specialised field Sumeriologists as

[1] Kramer, S. N., op. cit.

they came to be called, delved deeper and deeper into the origins of Sumerian civilisation, undistracted by the accretions of later cultures. New generations of archaeologists, from an increasing number of countries, dug and re-dug known sites and unearthed new ones; at the same time both linguists and archaeologists (sometimes the two were one) strove to interpret and understand the many texts, ranging from business and legal documents to religious and poetic literature, which had been scattered throughout the museums of the world. From time to time new hoards of the tablets were dug up, e.g. at Nippur by the American expedition under Dr. Peters.

No less important was the serious attempt to devise a scientific system of dating based on pottery-styles. "Sequence-dating" by pottery and other objects, initiated in Britain by General Pitt-Rivers and developed in the Near East by Sir Flinders Petrie was gradually applied to Mesopotamian sites. It is important to understand this technique, because otherwise the frequent references in books on Sumer to the "*al 'Ubaid* culture" and the Jemdet Nasr culture become meaningless and boring.

When dealing with relatively late cultures, e.g. Assyria, Persia, Greece, Rome, etc., the archaeologist is assisted by written documents and coins which enable him to date the objects he finds with reasonable precision. Herodotus has left a description of Babylon as it existed in the sixth century B.C. A Greek poet wrote about a Greek mercenary who fought in the army of Nebuchadnezzar. If a Roman coin bearing the name of Trajan dropped out of the pocket of a Roman soldier stationed in Alexandria, it is fairly obvious that the archaeological strata in which the coin is found cannot be earlier than the time of that Emperor. But as one penetrates further and further into the "time-tunnel" such clues become less and less frequent, until at last one approaches a region where there are no written documents, or if such documents do exist, there is no method by which they can be accurately dated. This is where "sequence-dating" comes in.

Pottery, used in abundance by the ancient peoples—for storing food, for cooking and other purposes—is virtually indestructible. It does not matter to the archaeologist that the pots have been shattered into scores of fragments. For these bits and pieces will bear the unmistakable marks of *style*, as indelibly imprinted as dates and names on a coin. And with each generation this style gradually changed. The impact of new peoples—invaders, perhaps, from another land—is usually marked by the introduction of their own characteristic style of pottery; therefore a cataclysmic revolution, a time of pillage and death and terror, the burning of cities and the massacre of a people may be indicated, on an ancient site, merely by the ashes of burned buildings, and the introduction of a different style of pottery. . . .

Archaeologists use the word "culture" to indicate a people, or group of peoples, who produced the same kind of artefacts. Thus if, on a Sumerian site in southern Mesopotamia, objects are found which are identical, or almost identical with those discovered on another site in Persia, hundreds of miles away, they must indicate some kind of relationship, e.g. that the ancestors of the Sumerians may have come from the highlands of Persia, or that they were conquered by invaders from that country. Also, by noting the strata in which such objects appear, the archaeologist can establish *comparative* dates, e.g. he can be reasonably certain that Stratum A is later than Stratum B, because the latter is below the former. And if, by some miraculous chance Stratum A contains some datable object he can be equally certain that if Stratum A objects turn up on another site they are roughly of the same date. Thus it becomes possible to build up a chronological system, so that a man may pick up a fragment of pottery and say, with confidence, "this was made between 2000 and 1800 B.C. by such-and-such a people."

*   *   *

After the extraordinary discoveries of de Sarzec at Telloh, German scholars were moved to emulation. Through the generosity of L. Simon the Royal Prussian Museums of Berlin were able to conduct excavations at Babylon in 1887. The archaeologists principally concerned were Dr. Robert Koldewey, Dr. Bernhard Moritz and Mr. Ludwig Meyer. They left Berlin in the autumn of 1886 and reached the site in the following spring. Babylon is an enormous site so the German archaeologists picked out two principal mounds for investigation, those of Surghul and El Hibba. Though they soon realised that the complete excavation of the sites was beyond their resources, they made trial trenches, discovered deep wells of terracotta rings, and innumerable funerary remains which Koldewey regarded as "fire necropoles" dating from a period "probably older than that of the earliest civilisations".

It was here that Dr. Koldewey—surely one of the greatest of excavators—received his training, on the site which he was later to make famous when, between 1900 and 1914, he painstakingly uncovered the Babylon of Nebuchadnezzar, creating "order out of chaos", carefully tracing every wall, revealing the Processional Way, the site of the "Hanging Gardens" and the Ishtar Gate which is now the pride of the Berlin Museum. But as this belongs to a relatively recent period of Mesopotamian history (c. 600 B.C.) it can only be briefly mentioned in the present volume.

Perhaps the greatest achievement of Dr. Koldewey, Dr. Andrae and other archaeologists of the *Deutsch-Orient Gesellschaft* was the technique of "wall tracing" which they developed and perfected. When a mud-brick city falls into ruin it is usually extremely difficult to distinguish between the original walls and the surrounding debris which tend to form an agglutinous mass. Often only a slightly darker line in the mud shows where the original walls were. Earlier excavators such as Layard, Loftus and Taylor tunnelled through walls and debris alike, concerned mainly with finding antiquities. But the sensitive, almost surgical method used by Drs. Andrae and Koldewey, which is now standard practice among competent archaeologists, enabled them to lay bare the whole complex plan of an ancient Mesopotamian city.

At Ashur, for instance, they achieved—

a brilliant feat of excavating, the prototype of all strati-
graphical investigatings of later times. It involved the
tracing, clearing, photographing and clearing away its
ruins and attending to its predecessor. Its reward was the
discovery of the Archaic Temple buried beneath the
deeply accumulated evidence of its great antiquity, and
providing for the first time detailed evidence of Sumerian
religious rites and the paraphernalia connected with them
in its original setting.[1]

America came later on to the scene, though already, between 1860 and 1870, American scholars had shown a keen
interest in Rawlinson's decipherment of the cuneiform, and
particularly in the publication by George Smith of the
Chaldaean Account of the Deluge. The works of Schrader were
studied as were Professor Sayce's *Assyrian Grammar* and the
Lesetücke of Delitsch. For a time the older American scholars
tended to be sceptical regarding the new science of Assyriology,[2] but eventually they were won over. David Gordon
Lyon, of Benton, Alabama, studied under Delitsch at Leipzig
and afterwards founded a new school of Assyriology in the
United States. His own publications, such as *Keilschrifttexte
Sargons* (Leipzig 1883) and his *Assyrian Manual* published in
Chicago in 1886 were considerable works of scholarship, and
did much to attract American students to this new field of
linguistics and archaeology.

Some Assyriologists went to America from Germany to
found new faculties in American Universities. Among these
were Hermann Vollrat Hilprecht and Paul Haupt. Hilprecht
distinguished himself later as one of the first Americans to
excavate in Mesopotamia. He served first under Dr. Peters at
Nuffar (ancient Nippur) to which the University of Pennsylvania sent an expedition in 1887. After some initial set-

[1] Lloyd, Seton, op. cit.

[2] At this period the separate discipline of Sumerology was unknown; the
study of cuneiform writing came under "Assyriology".

backs (including an armed Arab attack and the burning of
the Mission's camp) the expedition settled down to a sys-
tematic investigation of this huge site, and in due course
located the archive-rooms containing over 2,000 tablets and
numerous objects dating from the third millennium B.C. In
1890 another 8,000 tablets were found, and between 1893 and
1896 a further 20,000, when Mr. J. H. Haynes worked almost
alone at Nuffar. Later Hilprecht was made Director of Excavations, and Haynes, who worked under him, made a
series of splendid discoveries; the Library of the temple of
Enlil, containing 23,000 tablets, the sites of ancient Kisarra
and Shuruppak, and again at Nuffar. Of Haynes, Sir E. Wallis
Budge writes:

> Though neither an Assyriologist nor an expert archaeo-
> logist, for he was only attached to the Expedition as a
> photographer, all Assyriologists who study the texts found
> by him at Nuffar owe him a debt of gratitude.

It is mainly due to such men as Hilprecht and Haynes that
American universities now possess the finest collection of
cuneiform inscriptions in the world; to these writings we owe
much of our knowledge of the social, domestic, commercial
and religious life of the Sumerians.

American archaeologists also worked at Bismayah ("the
Lost City of Adab"). Frenchmen dug at Kish, L. W. King
re-examined the mound of Kuyunjik on behalf of the British
Museum. By the beginning of the twentieth century the
Turkish scholars also began to take a hand, after a long
period of indifference to the fate of pre-Islamic monuments.
Gradually a new freemasonry of scholarship began to develop which overrode national boundaries. Whereas in
Victorian times scholars of differing nationalities competed
with each other for the possession of antiquities, at the end of
the First World War, Dr. Koldewey was able to retrieve the
bricks of the Babylonian "Ishtar Gate" which had remained
safely stored throughout the war in the German expedition
house at Hillah. There they remained until 1926, when their

release to the German Government was sanctioned, and the rebuilt Gate of the Love Goddess now stands in the Berlin Museum.

Among those responsible for this new, liberal attitude to international scholarship was Miss Gertrude Bell, that distinguished traveller, writer and Orientalist whose book, *Amurath to Amurath*, reveals an equal awareness both of Mesopotamian antiquity and the cultural renaissance of the Arabs.

For the first time [she wrote] in all the turbulent centuries to which those desolate regions bear witness, a potent word had gone forth, and those who caught it listened in amazement, asking one another for an explanation of its meaning. Liberty—what is liberty? I think the question which ran so perpetually through the black tents would have received no better a solution in the royal pavilions which once spread their glories over the plain. Idly though it fell from the lips of the Bedouin it foretold change. . . .[1]

Change indeed; such a change as would have puzzled such pioneers as Rich, Layard and Loftus. After the First World War and the collapse of the old Ottoman Empire the indigenous inhabitants of Iraq began to assume control of their destinies. And while European and American scholars were still encouraged to dig in Mesopotamia, the Arabs who worked for them were no longer mere hired labourers but members of a proud race which had begun to re-establish dominion over its own territory. Moreover, with the militant nationalism characteristic of newly-enfranchised peoples, they sometimes became impatient with the activities of foreigners grubbing perpetually in the dust-heaps of the past.

"Oh Beg! you take much trouble to get one of these pots of the old *Kaffirs*—may they be cursed!" an Arab workman had said to Loftus in 1850. After 1918 the educated Arabs, forward-looking and conscious of their new independence, tended to make the same comment, but more forcefully.

[1] Bell, Gertrude. *Amurath to Amurath*, Wm. Heinemann, 1911.

Meanwhile, harrassed at times by new political problems but undeflected from his main purpose, the Sumeriologist continued to probe deeper into alluvial mud of Mesopotamia, seeking to "satisfy man's universal quest for origins—the 'firsts' in the history of civilisation".

CHAPTER EIGHT

THE ARCHAEOLOGIST AS DETECTIVE

FOR the Sumeriologist the period between the two World Wars provided a mounting climax to everything which had gone before. It was as if the discoveries of the earlier explorers were like isolated pieces of a gigantic jigsaw puzzle, some of which could be placed in conjunction,—while others remained isolated. Between 1918 and 1940 the pieces began to fit together, and—even more important—more pieces began to be found, and the picture acquired depth as the archaeologists found earlier and still earlier evidences of Sumerian origins.

For the present writer the fascination of this process is twofold. First, there is the hunt for "clues" in the form of pottery and other objects which reveal deeper and deeper strata of cultures; evidence of peoples who lived in western Asia and developed a high degree of civilisation centuries before the invention of writing. Archaeologists give this period several names, e.g. "prehistoric", "proto-literate", "proto-Sumerian", or "pre-Dynastic", i.e. before the times of the Dynastic kings of whom written records survive.

Second, there is the more obvious and spectacular appeal of buried splendour, of which the finest example was found by Sir Leonard Woolley in the "Royal Cemetery" at Ur. These wonderful finds, which will be described in Chapter 10 made the greatest impression on the general public, but since even the richest jewel acquires added beauty from its setting so the glories of Dynastic Ur may be best appreciated against the chronological background provided by "sequence-dating". Consequently, this and the following chapter will follow the trail of what one might irreverently call the "pot-hunters", the archaeologists who sought for Sumerian origins in the debris of buried cities in many places. This involves yet a deeper penetration of the "time-tunnel", taking us far away from Mesopotamia itself to other, more distant sites, from the highlands of Persia to the Mediterranean coast.

* * *

We take up the thread after the outbreak of the First World War, when Dr. Koldewey, after sadly consigning the Babylonian Gate of Ishtar (in packing-cases) to the German Expedition House at Hillah, returned to Berlin, and Mesopotamia became once again a battlefield. In 1918 Mr. R. Campbell Thompson, formerly of the British Museum, made soundings at Ur when serving on the intelligence staff of the British Army. He also dug at Eridu, using Indian troops. As a result of these soundings, the British Museum sent an expedition under Dr. H. R. Hall who worked during 1918–19 at Ur, Eridu and a small mound called al 'Ubaid, near Ur.

While excavating a Sumerian temple there, Hall noticed on another part of the site a scatter of hitherto unknown pottery. It was dark green in colour, hard-baked and covered with geometrical designs in black paint. Hall was intrigued by this, but as usual lack of funds prevented further excavation of the mound. Then, in 1922, the Director of the University Museum of Pennsylvania, Dr. G. B. Gordon, suggested to the British Museum that the two institutions join forces in order to send an expedition to dig in Mesopotamia. The proposal was accepted, Sir Leonard Woolley was appointed Director of the joint expedition, and the site chosen was Ur.

Standing on the summit of this mound [writes Woolley] one can distinguish along the eastern skyline the dark tasselled fringe of the palm-gardens on the river's bank, but to north and west and south as far as the eye can see stretches a waste of unprofitable sand. To the south-west the flat line of the horizon is broken by a grey pinnacle, the ruins of the staged tower of the sacred city of Eridu, which the Sumerians believed to be the oldest city on earth, and to the north-west a shadow thrown by the low sun may tell the whereabouts of the low mound of al 'Ubaid; but otherwise nothing relieves the monotony of the vast plain over which the shimmering heat-waves dance and the mirage spreads its mockery of placid waters. . . .[1]

Tell al 'Ubaid lies about four miles to the north of Ur. It was a low mound, not more than six feet above the plain, strewn with unfamiliar pottery.

We excavated the mound [continues Sir Leonard] and were somewhat taken aback to find how little work it required—everything lay quite close to the surface. Under a few inches of light dust mixed with potsherds came a stratum not more than three feet thick composed of hard mud in which were quantities of sherds of painted ware, flint and obsidian tools, and bits of reed matting plastered with clay mixed with dung or, less often, with a mixture of earth and bitumen; below this was clean water-laid soil. This was, in fact, an island of river silt which originally rose above the marshy plain and had been seized upon by immigrants who had erected on it their primitive hut dwellings of reeds plastered with clay. The village had later been deserted and the dust and potsherds of the topmost layer represented its ruins. . . .[1]

"Bits of reed matting . . . clay mixed with dung . . .";
nothing exciting here; nothing spectacular; no impressive buildings or fine grave-furniture. Yet the little mound of al 'Ubaid was as important in its way as the richly-furnished tombs of Ur with their gold-work and jewellery. Why? Because—to use Kramer's words, already quoted in an earlier

[1] Woolley, Sir Leonard. *Excavations at Ur*, Ernest Benn Ltd., 1954.

chapter—it helped "to satisfy Man's universal quest for origins—for 'firsts' in the history of civilisation".

Some years ago I flew south from Baghdad to Basra, on the Persian Gulf. This was before the Jet Age, when one still flew slow enough, and low enough, to see the landscape. At first one saw nothing save biscuit-coloured desert, patterned here and there by patches of bitumen, like scrofulous outbreaks on human skin. It was a frightening landscape, harsh, sinister and evil. I strained my eyes to catch sight of the mounds of Hillah (ancient Babylon) but saw nothing. Occasionally one could detect a criss-cross pattern of ancient irrigation canals scoring the plain, and sometimes a cluster of black Bedouin tents crouched in a *wadi*, until after a long time the landscape began to change. Instead of sand-clouds swirling up to 10,000 feet there was water . . . an enormous, widespreading expanse of brown water, from which the tips of palm-trees emerged, like green feather-dusters. As we flew lower to land the hot humid atmosphere seeped into the cabin. The male passengers (it was July) peeled off their jackets and opened their shirts. Lower still we flew, the aircraft wallowing in the waves of hot air which rose from the steaming swamplands below. Yet there were *people* living down there. One saw villages on islands rising out of the flood water, and fishing-boats moving under brown sails. At five hundred feet it was easy to see these villages clearly—the cluster of huts made from bunches of reeds, dotted about among the palm-groves. We were looking at the homes of the Marsh Arabs, people whose way of life approximated very closely to that of the primitive inhabitants of al 'Ubaid whose mud-and-reed huts Woolley had unearthed from the dry Mesopotamian plain, six thousand years after they had been deserted.

It had long been suspected that in ancient times the Persian Gulf reached much further north, that in fact it had extended north of Baghdad. Here was startling confirmation. Seven thousand or more years ago the whole of what is now southern Iraq had been under water.

Here at al 'Ubaid [writes Seton Lloyd] were people who

had appeared when the Gulf was beginning to recede. The silt brought down by the two rivers was changing the sea into marsh, and islands were beginning to appear above them, on which it was possible to live and plant corn.[1]

Since these were obviously the first people to settle on newly-claimed land, clearly they must have come from somewhere; but where? And were they the ancestors of the Sumerians? These questions could not be answered until further sites had been found and dug. Meanwhile this particular "culture" was named *al 'Ubaid*, after the site at which the characteristic pottery and implements of the period were first found. Soon another site was excavated, at Uqair, by Mr. Seton Lloyd. He found a well preserved example of an *al 'Ubaid* village with walls standing to a height of several feet and a main street wide enough to take a laden pack animal. The roofs had been flat, with terracotta drain-pipes of an almost exactly similar shape to the tin ones used by the villages of modern Iraq.

There were well-planned houses with staircases which had led to the roofs. There were ovens, in one of which the excavators found discarded shells of freshwater mussels. Both at Uqair and at al 'Ubaid itself there was plentiful evidence of fishing, as one would have expected. Net-weights were found, and harpoons, and models of boats with a high prow and stern, like the modern *bellum*. These people also hunted game with slings (stag's antlers were found), tilled the soil with primitive hoes, and reaped their crops with sickles of hard-baked clay. Some of their pottery was painted with spirited pictures of animals.

The only objects which might have had religious significance were a number of small clay figurines, possibly representing a deity. But no building was found which could be regarded as a temple.

Gradually other examples of this *al 'Ubaid* culture were found in other parts of Iraq and even as far away as the highlands of Persia, hundreds of miles away. By 1930 it had been

[1] Lloyd, Seton. *Twin Rivers*, Oxford University Press, 1943.

decided that these early colonists of what was later to be
Sumeria had come from the Persian highlands, either driven
out of their homeland or attracted by the fertile land which was
appearing above the Euphrates as the great river silted up. (The
period of settlement is believed to have been about 5000 B.C.) [1]

The next cultural stage was discovered by German
archaeologists at the same time that Sir Leonard Woolley
was digging at Ur. They found large monumental buildings of
mud-brick houses, temples, and even a shrine raised on a
platform—the precursor of the later staged towers or *ziggurats*. Here the German excavators also found examples of
what is now recognised as the characteristic architectural
decoration of this *Uruk period* (as it came to be called). This
consisted of thousands of little cones of baked clay, roughly
the shape of a rifle cartridge. The tips of these were painted
in various colours and the cones driven in to the mud-brick
wall, forming a charming mosaic pattern (see illustrations).
Originally these cones may have been invented to strengthen
the buildings, but later they were developed as an architectural adornment.

The late Professor Childe who, in the twenties, examined
the great pit which the Germans dug at Erech, describes it in
his book *New light on the Most Ancient East*.

> At Erech, Heinrich, Jordan and Nöldeke sank a great
> shaft over six feet deep from the ground level of a temple,
> itself still prehistoric but already possessing the essential
> features of a Sumerian sanctuary. The huge deposit cut by
> this pit consists entirely of the debris of prehistoric settle-
> ments. . . . As one winds down the shaft to virgin soil, five
> feet below the present level of subsoil water, one has before
> one a concrete conspectus of the prehistory of Sumer in the
> relics projecting from the walls of the shaft. Woolley at Ur
> obtained comparable data from three shafts, none of which

[1] It is a curious fact that the modern Marsh Arabs of southern Iraq
build semi-cylindrical huts of reeds, of which the entrances have a
peculiar arrangement of crossed reed-bundles. Similar huts are shown in
early Sumerian reliefs carved 5,000 years ago. L.C.

reached the heart of the prehistoric settlements as definitely as that at Erech. . . .

. . . At the very moment perhaps that the more favourable conditions of the pluvial period were giving way to the existing arid regime, the tract termed Sumer was emerging from the sea as the silt of the Tigris and Euphrates filled up the Persian Gulf. The fresh-water Lagoons and reedy marshes offered themselves as a refuge for the wild life of what was becoming a desert. And to the flood-watered islands of the marshes man followed his prey and found escape from the drought; the ruins of his reed huts are found only a few inches above the primeval mud of the Gulf bottom.[1]

Meanwhile Woolley was digging a deep shaft into the ruins of Ur.

At a certain point in the layers of debris [writes Seton Lloyd] the greenish *al 'Ubaid* pottery with its painted designs in black stopped. For several feet above not a single example of painted ware was to be found. Even more interesting, it had given way to an entirely different and alien pottery, red-black or grey in colour with a burnished or polished surface. This was precisely the character of the pottery which the Germans were now finding at Warka.[2]

Here we see the vital importance of the "sequence dating" technique. At Uruk the German scholars find buildings, houses, temples, in direct association with a certain type of pottery. At Ur Woolley finds the same type of pottery *above* the *al 'Ubaid* ware, which was already known to belong to colonists who settled among the reed-marshes of the Euphrates valley when, as the author of Genesis relates:

God said, Let the waters under the heaven be gathered together unto one place, *and let the dry land appear*;[3] and it was so.

[1] Childe, Gordon. *New Light on the Most Ancient East*, Kegan, Paul, Trench, Trubner and Co. Ltd., 1934.

[2] Lloyd, Seton, op. cit.

[3] Our italics.

Immediately above this stratum the British archaeologists find examples of what later comes to be called the *Uruk* style of pottery, giving comparative, though not absolute dating. Thus, when other examples of this *Uruk* ware turn up at other places in Iraq and beyond, it is positively known that such remains date from a period following that of the *al 'Ubaid* people.

But by far the most important contribution of the *Uruk* people—whoever they were—was the art of writing. We now know that writing began in Iraq and was later adopted by Egypt, and there are sufficient similarities between the two writing-systems—in their early stages—to make it certain that the Mesopotamian system came first. How the cultures, separated as they were by a vast distance, came into contact is not yet known with certainty. It may have been at a common meeting point in Syria, or possibly via the Red Sea and southern Arabia, along which from prehistoric times ran the "spice route" which provided the incense which burned both on Egyptian and Sumerian altars.

Among the "proto-Sumerians" of the *Uruk* phase writing began with a few marks on a clay tablet made with the end of a reed. Lloyd gives this example: "Supposing a servant has been entrusted by his master with three bags of corn to take to a nearby village he would need on arrival a record of what he had been given." At this period also we first find the typical Sumerian cylinder-seal (also found in Egypt at Naquada). The purpose of this was to provide a Sumerian official or merchant (who was probably illiterate) with a means of identification. The typical "cylinder-seal" was a large cylindrical bead inscribed with signs and/or a picture. From these seals, thousands of which have been found, a great deal has been learned about the details of Sumerian social, economic and religious life.[1]

From the original simple pictograms, in which a picture represented a word (as in Ancient Egypt) a complex writing-

[1] See *Cylinder Seals of Western Asia* by D. J. Wiseman, Batchworth Press, 1959.

system arose, in which the signs became more and more
formalised until what had originally been a recognisable
picture of an object—a bird or a fish, a donkey or an ox—was
reduced to a few wedge-shaped signs representing a syllable
of a word, and a sophisticated grammatical system arose
which was only gradually interpreted by generations of
European and American scholars, from Rawlinson onwards.

Dividing the so-called "predynastic", "proto-Sumerian"
or "prehistoric" period, i.e. before the time of written
chronicles, we find (a) the *al 'Ubaid* culture, and (b) the much
more highly-developed *Uruk* people who, from the alien style
of their pottery, their embryonic writing-system and sophisticated architecture, appear to have been newcomers
who superimposed superior culture on the marsh-dwellers of
the *al 'Ubaid* period.

Once again the question of origins arose. We have seen
how the *al 'Ubaid* people came from the highlands of Iran
(Persia). Where did the *Uruk* invaders originate? Eventually
it was proved that they came from what is now central
Turkey, where pottery of similar style and shape was found.
An intermediate stage in the passage of these *Uruk* people was
discovered in 1939 at the foot of the Sinjar Hills north-west of
Mosul.[1] There archaeologists of the Iraqui Government
found a pre-dynastic village where the typical grey *Uruk-
style* pottery lay above painted *al 'Ubaid* ware. Here again as
at Uruk, there was evidence of architectural skill and a feeling for scale and design; a single private house was excavated
which had doors with ornamental recesses and a pair of decorated niches on each side of a central chamber. These *Uruk*
people were metal-users too. A few examples of copper tools
had been discovered at al 'Ubaid but on the Uruk sites the
metal was used plentifully.

However, a gap still remained between the *Uruk* period
and that of the Dynastic kings, of whom elaborate written
records existed among the baked-clay tablets found by earlier
explorers. This gap was closed when Langdon of the British

[1] See *Iraq*, Vol. VII, Part I, Spring 1940.

Museum excavated a site called *Jemdet Nasr* near the ancient Sumerian city of Kish. Above the *Uruk* layer, with its plain pottery, appeared a layer of painted pottery, burnished, like *Uruk* ware, but using a characteristic lattice-work design reminiscent of baskets. The German excavators at Warka found confirmation of this "new" culture, not only in pottery-fragments but in some splendid sculpture. One of the treasures of the Iraq Museum is a life-sized marble statue of this period; there is also the famous carved stone vase adorned with sculptured reliefs showing servants bringing offerings to a king.

At this period, between that of the *Uruk* people and that of Dynastic Sumer, building had changed very little, but writing had improved considerably. Signs now represented a syllable rather than a word, and were more highly stylised. Each sign or group of signs was enclosed in a rectangle. Metal was now in common use. The excavators found chisels, daggers, and barbed fish-hooks very like those used in Mesopotamia today. The period approximated to the end of the fourth millennium—round about 3200 B.C.—the time at which the Pharaohs of the First Dynasty gained control of Egypt.

In fact the stage was set for the curtain to rise on the historic period of ancient Sumer, with its known kings such as *Ur-nammu* and *Mes-anni-pad-da*. And if this book was an historical romance or a play, the curtain would now be rung up with a resounding roll of drums. However, this is not fiction but an attempt to present facts. Like the detective who, at the brink of an apparent solution, finds a new and baffling set of clues, the reader must now be prepared to retrace his steps. Before he can go forward and see the glories of the Dynastic period, he must first go back again, this time to a period even earlier than that of *al 'Ubaid*.

CHAPTER NINE

MINGLED THREADS

THERE is no such thing as a "pure" race. Go far enough back in to the history of any people and one finds an intermingling of blood. It is true that once a culture has had time to put down roots it develops its own characteristic forms which are then jealously guarded as racial or national traditions. One may call oneself German, or French, or British or American, but in fact we are all of composite origin. So it was even with the Ancient Egyptians, and so it was with Sumer.

By 1931 it was possible for a conference of archaeologists, meeting at Leiden, in Holland, to standardise the names of the three main cultural periods which preceded that of historical or "Dynastic" Sumer. These, in order of modernity, are:

1. *Early Dynastic* (beginning of written records and kingly chronicles about 3000 B.C.)
2. *Jemdet Nasr* (development of writing)
3. *Uruk* (architecture; beginning of writing)
4. *al 'Ubaid* (the marsh-dwellers who migrated from the highlands of Persia).

As we have seen, each of these cultures acquires its name purely from that of the site on which its characteristic pottery and other artefacts were first found. Absolute dating of the last three is impossible, since written chronicles do not begin until the Early Dynastic period. However, there was still doubt in the minds of some scholars as to whether the so-called *al 'Ubaid* culture was indeed the earliest.

In the Mosul area, in northern Iraq, American and British archaeologists found traces of a people who had developed a high culture long before the *al 'Ubaid* people settled in the marshes of southern Mesopotamia. Actually pottery of the type found on these sites was already known from a place called *Tell Halaf*, near Nisibin on the Turco-Syrian frontier, which was excavated by the Baron Max von Oppenheim before 1914. However, owing to the confused stratifaction of this site, the pottery could not at that time be accurately dated. Then in 1931, at two places, Tepe Gawra and Arpachiyah, similar pottery turned up, in a context which made it clear that it antedated the *al 'Ubaid* culture. "Thus", writes Seton Lloyd, "year by year the beginnings of human life in Mesopotamia seemed to be thrown further and further back, and the science of prehistoric pottery became more and more absorbing."[1]

So now we have to add another name to our list, again in order of modernity:

1. *Early Dynastic*
2. *Jemdet Nasr*
3. *Uruk*
4. *al 'Ubaid*
5. *Tell Halaf.*

Characteristic of the *Tell Halaf* culture was polychrome pottery, beehive-shaped houses and primitive temples. By 1935 other examples of this cultural epoch had turned up in several places, and its origin was located in the foothills of the Turkish mountains. It seemed that the thread of Sumerian civilisation was woven of strands from several sources; e.g. from Persia (Iran), from central Turkey and from northern Syria. But could there have been a people even earlier than those of *Tell Halaf*? The British Museum sent an expedition to Nineveh and, deep beneath the foundations of the Assyrian palace, found primitive pottery *below* the *Tell Halaf* level. However they could not find any equivalent ceramics

[1] Lloyd, Seton, op. cit.

anywhere in Iraq or in the countries immediately adjacent to
it. The search continued, the British digging at Sakje Geuzu
in Turkey, and the Americans near Antioch. They dug down
to deeper levels, finding evidence of a *chalcolithic*, i.e. "copper-
using" culture between the ages of stone and bronze. The
Turkish site of Sakje Geuzu had already been excavated between 1907 and 1911 by Professor Garstang, who made a
deep sounding beneath the foundations of a Hittite palace and
found neolithic remains. Later investigations during the inter-
War period confirmed the truth of Garstang's predictions.

Then, in 1936, the same distinguished British archaeologist—now Professor of Archaeology at Liverpool University
—returned to Turkey and, with Mr. Seton Lloyd, selected
for investigation a hitherto unexplored mound near the town
of Mersin. It lies in the Cilician plain between the Taurus and
Amaunus mountains, at the north-east corner of the Mediterranean.

Mersin is a long way from Iraq, yet the discoveries made
there had a vital bearing on the origins of Sumerian civilisation. "It was an extraordinary archaeological phenomenon",
writes Lloyd, "this 75 feet hummock of earth beside a stream
on the outskirts of Mersin."

The mound was barely 600 feet in diameter at the base and
much less at the top. Both Garstang and Lloyd thought at
first that they would find only the superincumbent remains of
a series of dull Hittite villages, far later in date than that of
prehistoric Sumeria. When they began digging it seemed that
their forebodings were going to be fulfilled. They found first a
Hittite fortress of a mere 1500 B.C., and beneath this a succession of stone-walled Hittite settlements of a type already
well known to excavators in Turkey.

But about midway between the summit of the mound and
the stream the buildings began to be of mud-brick and
there was a complete change in the pottery. Here, among
the *liben* houses was the familiar *al 'Ubaid* pottery of south
Iraq, slightly modified in design as a result of the many

hundreds of miles which separated the two sites. There
were about four levels of *al 'Ubaid* material underneath,
and then another change.

Buildings began to appear, which had been destroyed in
some conflagration. . . . Their contents were largely intact
and merely covered by the debris which had fallen from
the roof. There was much pottery, for the most part a
hitherto unknown and purely local painted ware, but
amongst this were fragments of typical *Tell Halaf* painted
vessels and other objects which might equally have been
found at Archapiyah.

They found a well-preserved *Tell Halaf* fortress with a city
gate, square towers and a section of wall pierced with loop-
holes for defence. But what was most exciting was that this
city was "separated from virgin soil by some 30 feet of occupation debris, *all representing a civilisation earlier than anything
known in Mesopotamia*" [1] (our italics).

Time was getting short. It was 1938 and near the end of the
excavating season. Garstang had only time to sink a test-pit
below the *Tell Halaf* level. But it revealed a great deal. Below
the fortress were mud-brick buildings and painted pottery
which could be identified as a more primitive form of *Tell
Halaf* ware. Below this point everything changed again.
There were stone houses, and a new kind of pottery, and
flint implements.

Here, unfortunately [writes Lloyd] having before us and
easily accessible the material remains of the first known
human being to live in houses and make pottery, our
excavation season came to an end, and before another
could be begun the Second World War intervened. [2]

*   *   *

After the Second World War Mersin (the actual site is called
Yumüktëpe) was re-dug by Garstang, who has described the

[1] Lloyd, Seton, op. cit.

[2] Lloyd, Seton, op. cit.

results in his "Explorations in Cilicia" and *Prehistoric Mersin*.[1] He explored the lower-Neolithic settlements, finding flint weapons and implements and primitive pottery, very like that which he had already located in the deeper levels of Sakjeu Geuzu and at Jericho. At the most conservative estimate the earliest settlement at Yumüktëpe could not have been later than 4500 B.C., and above this lay the record of almost continuous development over a period of some five thousand years. First Man the hunter and shepherd; then Man the farmer and cultivator, storing his grain in silos; still later, Man weaving garments from spun wool and making metal tools and implements; in the Chalocolithic period there is evidence of communal organisation for defence, then more centuries of peaceful development, culminating in yet another defensive phase, when the Hittite fortress was built in about 1500 B.C.

All this evidence of some fifty centuries of human striving and effort lay buried under a mound of earth beside a clear stream near an unimportant town in Turkey.

It now becomes clear that the form taken by the civilisation which arose, some five thousand years ago in lower Mesopotamia, and which we now call Sumerian, was woven of many threads. There are still many gaps in the "jigsaw" puzzle, but a pattern can now be seen. A people, whom for convenience we call the *Tell Halaf* folk, had for many centuries established themselves in the hill-country of what is now northern Syria and southern Turkey. Gradually they moved into Iraq as far as the head of the Persian Gulf which then reached north of Baghdad. Meanwhile, in the neighbourhood of Mosul, even more primitive settlers had arrived, whom the *Tell Halaf* people probably superseded.

Next came a new wave of invaders from the east, the *al 'Ubaid* folk from the highlands of Iran; like the *Tell Halaf* people the newcomers used implements of stone and flint;

[1] Garstang, J. "Explorations in Cilicia", Liverpool Annals of Archaeology and Anthropology XXIV (1936, 1937, 1938) and *Prehistoric Mersin*, Clarendon Press, 1952.

they were farmers and stockrearers, skilled in many crafts, though their hand-made pottery style was a little less advanced. The deposits at Tepe Gawra and elsewhere show that it took a long time for the "pure" al 'Ubaid style of pottery to establish itself, so that it would appear that these people gradually became dominant over the Tell Halaf folk; there would be an intermingling of stocks. Meanwhile, further south, as the Gulf receded and the marshes dried out, new extremely fertile land was appearing, and the al 'Ubaid settlers were the first to occupy this. There, besides raising crops, they built boats and fished.

Eventually the al 'Ubaid folk were absorbed by yet a third wave of people, also mountaineers from Anatolia—the so-called Uruk people who used metal freely, had begun to use rudimentary writing and were skilful architects and town-planners. In the Uruk layers we find the first elaborate temples, and the beginnings of what was later to become the most characteristic feature of Sumerian religious architecture, the staged tower. The fact that these settlers originated from a mountainous country leads some archaeologists to believe that these towers were artificial "mountains". Dr. Henri Frankfort points out, in his Birth of Civilisation in the Near East:

> The significance of the ziggurats is revealed by the names which many of them bear, names which identify them as mountains. That of the god Enlil at Nippur, for example, was called "The House of the Mountain", "Mountain of the Storm", "Bond between Heaven and Earth". Now "mountain" used in Mesopotamia is a term so heavily charged with religious significance that a simple translation does it as little justice as it would to the word "Cross" in Christian, or the words "West" or "Nun" (primeval ocean) in Egyptian usage. In Mesopotamia the "mountain" is the place where the mysterious potency of the earth, and hence of all natural life, is concentrated.

Frankfort draws attention to a rough terracotta relief found at Assur in a temple of the second millennium B.C.

which shows a deity whose body grows out of the mountain-
side, while plants grow from his body and from his hands.
Goats feed on the plants, and water, indispensable to life, is
represented by two figures flanking that of the god. Similar
representations occur on cylinder seals of a much earlier date.

> Deities like the main figure of this relief [writes Frankfort]
> were worshipped in all Mesopotamian cities, although
> their names differed. Tammuz (Adonis) is the best known
> of them. As personifications of natural life they were
> thought to be incapacitated during the Mesopotamian
> summer, which is a scourge destroying vegetation and
> utterly exhausting man and beast. The myths express this
> by saying that the god "dies" or that he is kept captive in
> the "mountain". From the "mountain" he comes forth at
> the New Year when nature revives. . . . Thus the "moun-
> tain" is essentially the mysterious sphere of activity of the
> superhuman powers. The Sumerians created the condi-
> tions under which communication with the gods became
> possible when they erected the artificial mountains for
> their temples.[1]

Next came the *Jemdet Nasr* folk, who like the *al 'Ubaid*
people also came from Iran. With them writing develops
considerably, metal came into common use, and fine works
of stone appear. So the stage is set for the true Dynastic
Period, when written records begin.

In order to keep the chronological thread clear I have deliberately omitted from this chapter the wonderful finds
which Sir Leonard Woolley made at Ur in the twenties. But
now it is time to return to the great mounds of Ur, near which
the first evidences of the *al 'Ubaid* culture were found, and see
what the Sumerians, in whose culture so many diverse
threads were mingled, could produce in the Early Dynastic
Period.

[1] Frankfort, Henri. *Birth of Civilisation in the Near East*, Williams &
Norgate Ltd., 1951.

From the Babylon of Nebuchadnezzar Dr. Koldewey recovered
the magnificent Ishtar Gate. It has been restored and erected in
the Berlin Museum.

The Processional Way was one of the glories of Babylon. Although it and the Ishtar Gate belong to a more recent period (c. 600 B.C.) they are superb examples of the flower of Sumerian culture and must be included.

ABOVE: This greenish pottery with black painted design comes from the al 'Ubaid period and dates back to 5000 B.C. BELOW: This type of painted clay pot from the Jamdat Nasr period replaced the earlier style as new racial stock entered the valley.

Cylinder seals of the Royal Cemetery period.

Seal dedicated to Ur-Nammu. The two-columned inscription
shows that Hashamer dedicated his seal to Ur-Nammu, king
of Ur, *c.* 2050 B.C.

ABOVE: The excavation site of the Royal Graves at Ur. The terraces and steps in the site are the result of the differing levels of the 1,800 graves which were excavated. BELOW: Sir Leonard Woolley and his wife working on the still imbedded harps. They are scraping around the relics with a knife and blowing the soil away with a small bellows.

The harps (or lyres) from the first Royal Grave in their original
state, crushed and decayed by the weight of forty feet of earth
and only held together by compacted soil.

With skill and patience the wonderful harps were restored very
nearly to their original appearance.

Plan of the best preserved of the Ur death-pits. Sixty-four ladies of the court, four harpists and six men soldiers were laid out in this chamber.

ABOVE: Queen Shub-ad's boat-shaped gold bowl. BELOW: This elegant gold feeding cup was found near the entrance to Queen Shub-ad's grave.

The crushed and broken head-dress of Queen Shub-ad as it was when first uncovered. The pins and amulets are by the right shoulder at the left of the photograph.

This is the exquisitely-fashioned gold and jewelled head-dress after restoration, with the features modelled in wax by Lady Woolley.

This sculpture of a lady of the Early Sumerian period was set up in a temple to pray for the subject's welfare.

One of a series of statues representing Gudea, governor or king of the city of Lagash. The remarkable serenity and dignity make this one of the finest pieces of portrait sculpture of any time.

Plaque of Dudu the Scribe. The eagle and two lions at the
top are the symbol of the god Ningirsu. The young bullock
on the left is a symbol of plenty.

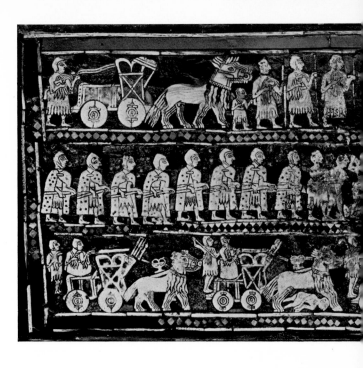

The mosaic Standard of Ur. The top panel represents scenes from war and gives a detailed picture of the Sumerian army.

The bottom panel, scenes from peace, shows the royal family feasting. The lower rows show attendants bring in food supplies.

The Ziggurat of Ur-Nammu.

CHAPTER TEN

BURIED SPLENDOUR

UR lies two hundred and twenty miles south of Baghdad, not far from the point where the great Shatt-el-Hai Canal runs into the Euphrates. The huge, sombre mounds of which the largest is called by the Arabs Tell el Muqayar—"the Mound of Pitch" [1]—rise from a desolate wasteland, "desert blank and unredeemed" as the late Sir Leonard Woolley describes it in his book *Excavations at Ur*. No one was better fitted and better able to describe this part of Iraq than Sir Leonard, who dug there for twelve successive seasons and who made the discoveries which, more than any others, revealed to the world the full splendour of Sumer. It is as romantic a chapter in the history of archaeology as the discovery in Egypt of the tomb of Tutankhamun.

Indeed, the major embarrassment of any contemporary writer attempting to describe Ur of the Chaldees is the persuasive beauty of Sir Leonard's style. It seems almost unfair that so talented an archaeologist should also be possessed of a romantic imagination and the gift of vivid self-expression. Turn to almost any page in the introductory chapters of *Ur Excavations* and one is captivated by passages like this:

... for more than half a century (after Taylor's excavations) there was a respite and Ur was left again to the jackals which have their earths in the tops of the Ziggurat and the wild pigeons which nest in the vent-holes in its

[1] Because of the bitumen used to bind its bricks together.

brickwork. . . . Today, after eleven successive seasons of excavation, Ur presents a very different spectacle. . . . Great spoil-heaps fill the hollows and run far across the level, trenches and cross-cuts mark the line of the town wall, and in the centre where was the Temenos or Sacred Area the old mounds have given place to a maze of walls and well-laid pavements of burnt brick. The Ziggurat stands out not as a shapeless heap it was but as a four-square tower whose brickwork might be that of yesterday, and its triple staircase still mounts as high as the lowest platform. . . .

But with the cemetery it is otherwise. Seen from the air its site is a patch of black shadow from which radiate the spoil-heaps where the trucks have dumped their contents along the ever-lengthening lines of light railway. From the ground, as one walks across the ruins of the Temenos one comes suddenly upon a precipice edge and looks down over a vast clearing some 220 feet by 170 in extent, dug down to a depth of 30 feet. . . . Sometimes in the face of an earth cliff there can be seen a clay pot or the broken end of a coffin which belonged to a burial lying on the cemetery's verge and has been noted and preserved *in situ*, but apart from such there does not remain a trace of the eighteen hundred private graves which were found within the limits of the pit's area; each in its turn was cleared and recorded and the objects lifted and carried off, and then it was dug through in order that the next below it might be brought to light . . . Hamoudi's[1] pious gratitude did indeed preserve the grave of Mes-kalam-dug, a mere rectangular depression in the top of an earth column, and one can still trace the outlines of the Great Death-Pit. . . .

But, as Sir Leonard sadly observes:

Grave-digging is necessarily destruction, and because that is so the grave-digger incurs a heavy responsibility. The buildings which we unearth remain as a visible record or,

[1] Hamoudi was Sir Leonard Woolley's Arab foreman.

if need be, could be dug out a second time to furnish evidence overlooked or misinterpreted, but, with a cemetery, when once the work is done it is impossible to check or amplify the observations made at the time; consequently the record must be full, and if others are to have fair grounds for forming their own conclusions as to the meaning of things it must be fully published.[1]

This Donne-like awareness of man's fragile mortality, and of the atmosphere of "pleasing melancholy" which clings to an ancient site, is instinctive in Sir Leonard's writing; yet all is controlled and conditioned by cool scientific observation and a strict regard for truth. I offer no apology, therefore, if a substantial part of this and the following chapter reveals the glories of Ur not through my eyes, but those of the man who first saw them.

Among the innumerable written documents of the historic period, there is a "King-List" which purports to give the names and lengths of reign of the ancient monarchs of Sumer and Babylonia. The earlier part, which concerns Sumer and Akkad, is reprinted as an Appendix to this volume. It is a curious document, and for a long period scholars were sceptical about it, especially the earlier section which gives the names of "Kings before the Flood". This, as will be seen, comprises eight kings, whose combined reigns total 241,200 years! The first king, *A-lu-bim*, of the city of Nun, is alleged to have ruled for 28,000 years, but even he is outdone by *En-me-en-lu-an-na*, who reigned for 43,000 years. After these first eight kings the chronicle says, briefly:

The Flood came. After the Flood came, kingship again was sent down from on high.

After the Flood, which, as we have seen in Chapter Three, is described in the Epic of Gilgamesh, comes the First Dynasty of Kish, with twenty-three kings reigning for 24,510 years, but with the following Dynasty, that of Erech (Uruk) the reigns of the later kings are of reasonable length, e.g.

[1] *Ur Excavations*, op. cit.

Ur-Nungal (30 years), Utul-kalamma (15 years) and Me-lam-an-na (6 years). The same is true of the following Dynasty, that of Ur, with King Mes-ani-ni-pad-da (80 years), Mes-ki-ag-Nannar (36 years) and so on.

Unlike the Dynasties of Egypt, these Sumerian Dynasties are associated with particular cities; e.g. Ur, Kish, Lagash, Erech. Thus was the *First* Dynasty of Kish followed by the *First* Dynasty of Erech; the *First* Dynasty of Ur is succeeded by the *Second* Dynasty of Kish. Then, after the Dynasty of Hamasi comes the *Second* Dynasty of Erech and the *Second* Dynasty of Ur. Although the intention seems to have been to suggest that these monarchs ruled the entire land, in fact some of them may have ruled from their separate cities contemporaneously. There were also Governors (*patesi*) of whom we have already met one example, Gudea of Lagash. The whole chronology of Dynastic Sumer is extremely complex, nor does its literature always help, because archaeologists have revealed the existence of personalities and religious customs which are not mentioned in the written documents.

But to return to Ur; when Sir Leonard Woolley led his combined Anglo-American expedition there in the early twenties, he had been told that he

> might expect to recover monuments taking us back so far in time as the reign of King Ur-Nammu, founder of the Third Dynasty of Ur, but should probably find nothing earlier. King Ur-Nammu was indeed almost the first character in the history of Mesopotamia to be acknow-ledged by scholars to be historically authentic; there were in museums actual monuments of earlier kings with their names written on them, but there was no means of saying when they reigned. . . .[1]

However, in quite an early stage of their excavations, the Expedition had a piece of luck. Near the mound of al' Ubaid they found the remains of a temple of the First Dynasty of Ur. Digging there one day—

[1] Woolley, Sir Leonard. *Excavations at Ur*, Ernest Benn Ltd., 1954.

a workman unearthed before my eyes a small oblong tablet of white limestone bearing an inscription; I handed it to Mr. Gadd, who was standing beside me, and he read it out: "A-anni-pad-da King of Ur, son of Mes-anni-pad-da King of Ur, has built this for his Lady Nin-Kharsag."[1] It was the foundation-stone of the building, and the most important of all our discoveries.[2]

The first name was unknown, but the second, Mes-anni-pad-da, was familiar as the first king of the First Dynasty of Ur, according to the Sumerian King-Lists. The importance of this discovery was that it established the reality of a dynasty which had been regarded as purely mythical; and it did more than this. It dated the building in which it was found, so that, henceforth, all objects associated with it could be given their correct place in the development of art in Mesopotamia. Only archaeologists can appreciate fully how important this is. It gives them a datum-line.

There is only space to describe briefly the other objects found in or near this temple; the four copper bulls, the copper reliefs which had adorned the walls of the sacred building, the inlaid columns with their *tesserae* and the mosaic friezes showing doves and cows. The latter frieze, Woolley suggests, may represent priests preparing the milk of the Mother-Goddess Nin-Kharsag "which was the nourishment of Kings". Earlier Dr. Hall found, on the same rich site, a great relief of eagles and the copper foreparts of lions which had once formed part of a ceremonial gateway. But the temple had evidently been sacked by enemies. For instance, certain architectural features such as two mosaic columns and two others sheathed in copper had been violently flung down. The spoilers had, in Woolley's words, "collected the bull statues in a heap, and then had undercut the walls and toppled them over". Again and again, in examining ancient sites, one finds evidence of violent destruction.

At the time of discovery this temple of the Mother Goddess

[1] A Goddess.
[2] Woolley, op. cit.

at al 'Ubaid[1] was the oldest in the world, and it was possible to reconstruct its original appearance. It is still unique as the best illustration of the art and architecture of the First Dynasty at Ur.

Wonderful as it was, the temple of the Goddess Nin-Kharsag cannot compare with the sepulchres of her devotees, which the Expedition was later to discover in the city of Ur itself. To appreciate these to the full one must read again Sir Leonard's book, *Excavations at Ur*, Chapter III, or, better, the superbly illustrated official publication (in two mighty volumes) *Ur Excavations; the Royal Cemetery*.[2] As a work of international scholarship it is unique. As a romance it outrivals the most fantastic of fairy-tales. And, like some fairy-tales, it is a mixture of beauty and horror.

The discovery was not made until 1927, five years after Woolley commenced his excavations. Although the archaeologist already suspected that rich treasure might exist at this spot (he had already found, in the area, graves containing gold beads) he deliberately delayed digging there until the workmen had been properly trained.

> We had a force of very wild Arab tribesmen, few of whom had ever handled tools before; they were completely ignorant, had no idea of what good workmanship was, were reckless and . . . dishonest. Moreover they were ignorant too. . . . Our object was to get history, not to fill museum cases with miscellaneous curios, and history could not be got unless both we and our men were duly trained. So I stopped work on the "gold trench".[3]

But there was another and more vital reason for postponing the work. As Woolley explains:

[1] The temple unearthed at al 'Ubaid must not be confused with the al 'Ubaid *period* discussed in earlier chapters. The temple belongs to historic times, more than fifteen centuries after the al 'Ubaid people first settled in southern Mesopotamia.

[2] *Ur Excavations, the Royal Cemetery*; by L. Woolley. Oxford University Press, 1934.

[3] *Ur Excavations*, op. cit.

... very little indeed was known of Mesopotamian archaeology, so little that the objects from these graves were vaguely dated by such authorities as I could consult to the Neo-Babylonian or, as more probable, to the Persian period, and though I could form no alternative theory I felt that this was doubtful in the extreme. . . . The more rich the cemetery proved to be the more necessary it was to leave it alone until external evidence had given us a more or less definite chronology.[1]

At the beginning of 1927 the workmen were disciplined and experienced. Under their skilled foremen, Yahia and Ibrahim Hamoudi, they had developed a high technical skill both in digging and in the preservation of fragile objects of antiquity. The site chosen was a cemetery which lay inside the Temenos (wall) of a temple built by Nebuchadnezzar at the comparatively recent period of c. 600 B.C. This, however, proved to be much larger than the Temenos which enclosed the earlier Dynastic city of Ur. In fact the Expedition soon discovered that it was sinking its shaft into an ancient rubbish-mound which had lain just outside the city walls (though *within* the enclosure of the much later Babylonian temple). With that gay abandon which still characterises some Oriental people today, the inhabitants of Ur in about 3000 B.C. had hurled their rubbish over the wall of the temple enclosure into the wasteland outside, so that in time the accumulated debris formed a *talus* or ramp. But as this area adjoined the great temple, and therefore had sacred associations, the deep pile of rubbish began to be used as a cemetery. In fact there were two cemeteries, one above the other, belonging to different peoples.

The graves found in the upper part, of which there were over 1,800, were fairly simple and contained little of intrinsic value. The typical grave was a simple rectangular pit in which the corpse was laid wrapped in matting or in a coffin of clay, wood or basket-work. The body always lay on its side, in the position of sleep, with the back straight or

[1] *Ur Excavations.* op. cit.

slightly curved, and the hands placed in a position in front of the breast and almost level with the mouth. Such burials, as Woolley points out, are "wholly unlike the rigid straightness of the al 'Ubaid dead or the tightly-contracted 'embryonic' position which marks the *Jemdet Nasr* graves." [1]

In none of these graves was found a single representation of a god although the provision of simple objects, reflecting the social status of the dead, suggests that there was a belief in some sort of after-life. But there were no religious symbols even of the most primitive kind. Most, though not all, of these simple graves had been robbed, but, most significantly, there was evidence of deep holes and tunnels sunk by professional tomb-robbers who were evidently in search of richer prey. "We found" writes Woolley, "circular shafts ... driven down vertically to the level of the (royal) tombs but some distance from them and then turning horizontally to tunnel towards the tomb they proposed to plunder." As in Egypt, the burrowings of the ancient tomb-robbers often provide the modern archaeologists with vital clues to the whereabouts of an important sepulchre.

Among the "private" graves one of the finest was that of a gentleman with the unattractive name of Mes-kalam-dug. His skull still wore a magnificent golden helmet, and beside him lay the remains of a bossed shield, gold-mounted daggers, bowls of silver, copper and stone. A gold dagger had hung from the waist of the skeleton; in front of its waist was "a solid mass of lapis and gold beads, hundreds in all" and the bony hands still clasped a bowl of heavy gold. Nothing comparable to this had been discovered by such pioneers as Rich, Layard and Loftus, yet even the grave of Mes-kalam-dug was overshadowed by what was to follow. "Had the royal tombs not been discovered," Woolley writes, "it would probably have been hailed as a king's grave; as it is, its wealth only emphasizes the difference between it and them."

---

[1] Such distinctions are important, since they indicate vital differences of religious custom, and therefore, usually, distinct peoples.

The discovery of the first "Royal" grave,[1] happened near the end of the 1926 season. The excavators came upon a shaft, much deeper than the others, at the foot of which lay a splendid gold dagger, with a hilt of lapis-lazuli and a golden sheath. There was also a hoard of copper weapons and a set of little toilet instruments, contained in a reticule. "Nothing like these things" Woolley writes, "had ever before come from the soil of Mesopotamia; they revealed an art hitherto unsuspected and they gave promise of future discoveries outstripping all hopes."[2]

Though the tomb had obviously been robbed, the presence of these lovely things, overlooked by the plunderers, was a sufficient indication of its original richness. Woolley and his patient staff must have been pleased that their forebearance to excavate this area in 1922 had given time for the adequate training of the Arab workmen. These had become so skilled that, in Sir Leonard's words:

Of course their main incentive is money, but they can be taught to take a more or less disinterested pride in doing a job well—that is for them a totally new experience, but they appreciate it . . . they know that our object is not treasure hunting but a search for some mysterious knowledge, and a workman digging in a barren spot where the chances of baksheesh are nil may be heard to comfort himself with the muttered phrase "this is in the interest of science", not knowing what science is. The best of them acquire a very great manual dexterity in the use of the entrenching-tool and the knife and will seldom do damage to the most delicate object. . . . They will call the neighbouring pickmen in to discuss the meaning of a change of soil and will be ready with theories based for the most part on an extraordinary visual memory of what has been found in past seasons—some will even identify the name on an inscribed brick or by the style of brickwork date a building.[3]

[1] The reason for the quotation marks will appear later.
[2] Woolley, Sir Leonard. *Ur of the Chaldees*, Penguin Books.
[3] *Ur Excavations*, op. cit.

The next important discovery, though less spectacular, was scientifically valuable. Lower Mesopotamia is a stoneless land. The nearest hills from which stone can be quarried are several hundred miles away. Yet, in digging into another deep shaft, the archaeologists came upon slabs and blocks of limestone forming a kind of paving. "To find stone blocks at such a depth was astonishing. Could they be, perhaps, the roof of a tomb? Woolley had to wait until the next excavating season before finding out."[1]

It was indeed a stone-built tomb at great depth, but, apart from a few scattered fragments of a gold diadem, was empty. A long tunnel leading from the sepulchre to ground level told the archaeologist why. Robbers, who knew the whereabouts of the tomb, had been there several thousand years before them. But, undeterred, the Expedition continued to dig, spurred on by that secret hope of all archaeologists, of finding a sepulchre which the ancient plunderers had somehow overlooked. It had happened once, in Egypt, when Howard Carter found the almost intact tomb of the Pharaoh Tutankhamun. Could it happen again, in the mounds of a Sumerian city?

The scorching Mesopotamian sun burned down on the Arab workmen as they delved deeper and deeper into the pit. The basket-boys chanted as they swung their loads, and the trucks on the little Decauville railway clattered further and further away from the site, dumping their cargo of debris, while Woolley, Lady Woolley, Mallowan and the rest studied plans, scrutinised potsherds and looked down, from the lip of the great shaft, on the bent backs of the labourers. When, as often happened, Hamoudi or one of the other Arab supervisors called for expert opinion on a find, some of the Expedition's British or American staff would scramble down into the dusty pit and, with sweat-filled eyes, delicately scrape away the soil from some fragile object, then make notes, sketches and photographs.

[1] Cottrell, Leonard. *Lost Cities*, Robert Hale, 1957.

Then came a discovery more strange and awe-inspiring
than any archaeological find of the past century, apart
from the tomb of Tutankhamun. . . . One day Woolley
came upon five bodies lying side by side in a shallow
sloping trench. This was not near the plundered tomb, but
some distance away. Below them was a layer of matting.
Tracing this along Woolley found another group of bodies.[1]

Those of them women carefully arranged in two rows;
they wore head-dresses of gold, lapis lazuli and elaborate
bead necklaces, but they too possessed no regular tomb
furnishings. At the end of the row lay the remains of a
wonderful harp, the wood of it decayed but its decoration
intact, making its reconstruction only a matter of care . . .
across the ruins of the harp lay the bones of the gold-
crowned harpist. . . .[2]

Further along the same sloping pit were animal bones, the
remains of a sledge-chariot decorated with golden lions, and
a mosaic of blue, white and red stones. Near the bones, which
were of asses, lay two human skeletons, clearly the grooms
who had led them into the pit. Yet none of these bones, and
their accompanying treasures, were in a built sepulchre such
as the Expedition had already found. They were simply laid
along the bottom of an earth trench which had subsequently
been refilled. As the archaeologists removed this earth filling
they were astonished by the richness and beauty of the objects lying beside the bodies. There was an inlaid gaming-
board, a set of chisels and a gold saw, copper vessels, wooden
chests adorned with lapis-lazuli and lovely vessels of volcanic
glass, gold, silver and marble.

. . . tall slender silver tumblers nested one inside the other;
a similar tumbler of gold, fluted and chased, with fluted
feeding-bowl, a chalice, and a plain oval bowl lay piled
together, and two magnificent lion's heads of silver, perhaps ornament of a throne. . . . The perplexing thing was

[1] *Lost Cities*, op. cit.

[2] *Ur of the Chaldees*, op. cit.

that with all this wealth of objects we had found no body so far distinguished from the rest to be that of the person to whom all were dedicated; logically our discovery, however great, was incomplete.[1]

After a century of excavation in Mesopotamia, objects were coming to light at Ur the like of which had never been seen before. As the Press of the world began to fill with stories of buried splendour, Woolley and his Expedition realised that even more wonderful discoveries might yet be made.

[1] *Ur of the Chaldees,* op. cit.

CHAPTER ELEVEN

THE DEATH-PITS OF UR

DURING subsequent seasons a number of these macabre sepulchres were found, but as, unlike the tombs of Ancient Egyptian kings and queens, they were often built on top of each other, it required great skill and care to separate them. For example, the earth ramp containing the bodies of women and asses led to an intact tomb containing the body of a woman, *Shub-ad*, whom Woolley dignifies with the name of Queen. But her tomb-chamber was not discovered until the excavators had penetrated to yet another stone-built sepulchre underneath hers. This had belonged to a man, *A-bar-gi*, who was identified by a cylinder seal inscribed with his name. However, his tomb had been plundered, though the robbers had left behind two model boats, one of copper, the other of silver. The significance of these is not certain. In Ancient Egypt the Pharaohs of the Old Kingdom were usually buried with full-sized boats which may have been intended to convey them, after death, to the sacred city of Abydos.[1] These Sumerian model boats may also have had some religious significance, though there is nothing in the texts to support this theory.

Yet the approach-ramp to A-bar-gi's tomb yielded even more treasures than that of Shub-ad. At the foot of the ramp lay the skeletons of six soldiers, in two ranks, their spears beside them and copper helmets on their crushed skulls.

[1] Or across the sky with the sun-god, Re.

Lower down the ramp were the remains of two ox-drawn wagons with the bodies of the drivers lying beside them. Still further down was a stone-built chamber. Against its outer wall lay the bodies of nine women who had been richly clothed in brightly-coloured robes. On their heads were splendid gala head-dresses of lapis-lazuli and carnelian, from which hung large gold pendants in the shape of beech-leaves. These ladies had also worn large gold earrings, silver hair-ornaments, and necklaces of gold and lapis.

The whole space between them and the wagons [writes Woolley] was crowded with other dead, women and men, while the passage which led along the side of the stone (tomb) chamber was lined with soldiers carrying daggers, and with women. . . . On top of the bodies of the "court ladies" against the chamber wall had been placed a wooden harp . . . by the side of the wall of the pit was a second harp, with a wonderful bull's head in gold, its eyes, beard and horn-tips of lapis-lazuli, and a set of engraved shell plaques not less wonderful; there are four of them, with grotesque scenes of animals playing the parts of men, and while the most striking feature about them is that sense of humour which is so rare in ancient art, the grace and balance of the design and the fineness of the drawing make these plaques one of the most instructive documents we possess for the appreciation of the art of early Sumer.[1]

Above the plundered tomb of A-bar-gi the Expedition came upon another stone chamber—the one approached by the ramp containing the ass-drawn sledge chariot. Naturally they expected to find it in the same state as that of the one below. But to their astonishment it was not. By some miracle the ancient tomb-robbers, who had partly rifled the approach ramp, had either overlooked or been prevented from reaching the main sepulchre. It was intact.

[1] *Ur of the Chaldees*, op. cit.

The chamber [writes Woolley] lay $5\frac{1}{2}$ feet below the level of its death-pit, i.e. its roof was flush with that of the pit's floor . . . inside the chamber a wooden bier stood somewhat askew across the north-west end; on it lay the body of Queen Shub-ad [identified by an inscribed cylinder found in the filling of the shaft]. She lay quite straight on her back, her head towards the west, her hands crossed over her stomach; a woman attendant was crouched by the side of the bier, near the head, and a second at the foot. There was no sign of any coffin, neither wood nor matting was found above the queen's body, and the framework of her bier was perfectly distinct and unmistakable as such.[1]

Sir Leonard then goes on in great detail to describe the regalia worn by the Queen, which was "most magnificent; it was in effect a more splendid and elaborate version of the court head-dress worn by the women whose bodies were found in the royal tombs in attendance on its principal occupant".

Could the most sophisticated Paris *modiste* have invented— for the modern *elegante*—anything more dizzily delightful than this creation of 5,000 years ago? Around the slender neck is a simple necklace of gold and lapis beads suspending a delicate gold medallion. Above, an enormous black wig frames the face, and provides the substructure for the head-dress itself. First there is a linked chain of golden rings hanging over the brow. Above that a row of delicate gold pendants, each shaped like a beech-leaf, encircles the forehead, and still higher, resting on the crown of the wig, is a veritable flower-garden; "gold 'willow-leaf' pendants tipped with carnelian, and between the leaves gold flower-rosettes whose petals were inlaid with lapis and white paste". Finally, crowning the whole glorious confection rose

a tall 'comb' of gold; it seems to have been set so as to lean slightly forward and its seven points ending in rosettes of

[1] *Ur Excavations; the Royal Cemetery*, op. cit.

gold with lapis centres were bent so as to droop over the crown of the head. Below the ears hung enormous gold ear-rings . . . fixed in the hair. . . .[1]

Clive Bell, in defining the word "civilisation" has pointed out that it does not bear any necessary relationship to such relatively modern conceptions as hygiene and humanitarianism. By his definition—with which I agree—the Italy of the Borgias was civilised, whereas other more "humane" periods were not. The age which produced the head-dress of Queen Shub-ad was supremely civilised. Indeed so far as feminine fashion—always a useful yardstick—is concerned, I consider that it was well abreast of our own.

The upper part of Shub-ad's body was covered by a mass of gold beads, silver, carnelian, agate, chalcedony and lapis-lazuli. A gold cup of the finest design lay near her hand. Who was this lady, and how had she looked in life? Lady Woolley, a talented artist as well as an archaeologist, modelled a wax head on the skull of a Sumerian woman found in one of the "death-pits", since the skull of Shub-ad herself was too badly crushed to be capable of reconstruction. In this skilful remodelling Lady Woolley was careful to preserve the bony structure of the face and the marks on the bones of muscular adhesions.

> The result was, in the opinion of Sir Arthur Keith [the distinguished British anatomist] an accurate representation of the Sumerian type; incidentally it is a type occasionally seen amongst the Arab women of southern Iraq today.[2]

It is this face which we see beneath the head-dress of Queen Shub-ad and so, as far as it is possible to recall her, this long-dead Queen may have looked as she swept through the staterooms of her Palace, accompanied by other ladies, similarly though less gorgeously attired.

No less than sixteen of these so-called "Royal Graves"

[1] *Ur Excavations; the Royal Cemetery*, op. cit.
[2] *Ibid.*

were found at Ur, though most had been partially robbed. All had one feature in common. There was a stone-built chamber, containing the body of the most important occupant. Adjoining this sepulchre there was also a "death-pit" a sloping ramp leading down to the tomb. On these ramps a considerable number of human beings, men and women, had lain down and given up their lives. In no tomb was there any evidence of violent death. Beside each body usually lay a little metal cup, and sometimes the archaeologists found a large metal vessel which may have contained the poison or narcotic with which these splendidly apparelled men and women—perhaps officers and men of the royal guard, royal concubines, and ladies-in-waiting to the queen—had ended their lives.

Among primitive peoples, even down to quite recent times, human sacrifice has been practised, sometimes as the accompaniment to a royal burial, often as part of a fertility-cult in which human life was offered to the gods in the hope of ensuring a good harvest. Of the latter type there are frequent examples in Greek mythology. Of the former, Ancient Egypt can furnish examples in the Early Dynastic period, around 3000 B.C. I recall seeing, around a First Dynasty mastaba-tomb at Saqqara in Egypt, a large number of small cells surrounding the main sepulchral chamber of a Queen. In each of these cells was a cluster of human bones, accompanied by objects appertaining to the dead man's trade—butcher, ship-builder, painter, or maker of stone vessels. These men had been ritually sacrificed at the burial—craftsmen who would serve the dead woman in the after-life.[1]

But the people whose bodies were found in the Ur death-pits were not artisans. The rich garments and elaborate jewellery of the women, the military accoutrements of the men, the splendidly-mounted chariots and wagons—all suggest that these were people of rank, and that they had gone to their deaths voluntarily. An elaborate religious ceremony

[1] This custom was abandoned very early in the historical period of Ancient Egypt. It does not occur after 2800 B.C.

must have taken place before the interment, with much music and chanting. In one case, recorded by Woolley, the harpist had continued playing to the last, her fingers still outstretched across the strings of her instrument. In another grave it was clear that, after the attendants had become unconscious, people had entered the death-pit, killed the animals and placed the harp *above* the inert body of its player. Most extraordinary and touching of all is the story of the silver head-band worn by one of these "court ladies".

In a third death-pit there had been a holocaust of victims, sixty-four women and six men. The bodies of the women lay in ordered rows, the heads of one row across the legs of the next. Each of the female attendants or "court ladies" (Woolley's phrase) had worn a silver head-band. The silver had been destroyed by the chemical action of the soil, but remains of the decomposition remained near the skulls. But one lady wore no head-band. This puzzled Woolley for some time until he found, near the body but not on the skull, what first seemed to be a metal cylinder. On careful examination in the laboratory, however, it proved to be a silver head-band tightly rolled up. Evidently this lady had arrived in the pit with the rolled-up headband in a pocket of her robe, intending to put it on later. For some reason she never did this, and the little metal cylinder remained beside her body until found 5,000 years later by the archaeologists.

*   *   *

We now have to consider a number of knotty problems raised by the discoveries in the Ur cemeteries, and particularly by the so-called "Royal" cemetery. First, into what slot do they fit chronologically? In what relation do they stand to the "proto-Sumerian" or "pre-historic" periods— *al'Ubaid, Uruk, Jemdet Nasr*? Secondly, can any of the names of the people buried in these tombs be identified with those in the Sumerian "King-Lists"? If not, who were these people, and despite their rich tomb-furnishings and elaborate burials, can they really be considered Kings and Queens?

Let us take first the question of chronology. There were two cemeteries one above the other. The upper one could be dated, from cylinder seals found in the graves, to the period of Sargon of Akkad (about 2400 B.C.). The main part of the lower cemetery (which had been dug in the old rubbish-tip outside the temenos wall) was made after the *Jemdet Nasr* period but before the beginning of the First Dynasty. In the bottom layers of this early cemetery the Expedition came upon a few *Jemdet Nasr* graves, and among the millions of pottery fragments contained in the rubbish-dump were many representing this culture, proving that the bulk of the graves were necessarily later.

The answer to the second question is "No". Not one of the distinguished personages found in the "Royal" tombs bears a name which can be identified from the King-Lists. We shall look in vain, in those lists, for such people as A-bar-gi and Shub-ad. Were they, then, kings and queens at all? Or could their obvious importance have arisen from another cause? Scholars are still divided on this question, some supporting Woolley's firm belief that these were the tombs of kings and queens who ruled Ur before the First Dynasty; others hold different beliefs, of which the most widely-held is the "Sacred Marriage" theory.

Mr. Sidney Smith, in the *Journal of the Royal Archaeological Society*, October 1938, suggested that

> the tombs might be more properly connected with the *gigunus*, mysterious underground structures mentioned in various texts, situated apparently near the gates of the sacred part of the city, that the principal occupant of the tomb was not a king but a priest or priestess who took the leading part in a . . . mystery-play celebrating the marriage of the god, and that the other corpses were those of people sacrificed not to him but with him to promote the fertility of the land.[1]

We know from much later Babylonian religious texts that

[1] "Ur Excavations," op. cit.

such "sacred marriages" did take place, usually on New Year's Day, when a priest and priestess, representing a god and goddess, mounted to the sacred chamber on the topmost level of the *ziggurat*, and there consummated the sexual act, as a result of which the fertility of the land was to be renewed. Such customs are well-known among other ancient civilisations, and after the ceremony the principal participants were usually sacrificed. In another version given by Herodotus concerning the principal temple of Babylon, a beautiful virgin spent a night alone in the sacred chamber and was visited by the god.

A year after the appearance of Smith's article Professor F. Bohl put forward the same theory in the *Zeitschrift für Assyriologie*, N. F., V (xxxix). Though this was based partly on misconceptions which Bohl himself corrected when he visited the site.

There are many arguments for and against the "Sacred Marriage" theory. Although Sumerian texts mention such a ceremony, they do not describe any killing of the participants. On the other hand neither do they describe human sacrifice in connection with a king's funeral, but this, as Woolley observes, is not surprising since no Sumerian account of such a funeral exists. And he goes on:

> The argument *ex silentio* militates far more against the Sacred Marriage theory than against that of Royal Tombs. Further, in a "sacred marriage" rite the bride of the god may be killed, but the man who impersonates the god is not likely to be similarly treated, and if with Sidney Smith we can fairly infer that in the celebration at Lagash "Gudea as the city governor played the part of Ningirsu" we can be sure that Sumerian custom made no such demand; Gudea had no intention of dying on that occasion and did not die. Had both bride and bridegroom been sacrificed they would certainly have been buried together, but in no tomb chamber do we find two principal bodies. Had the bride been sacrificed we should have found only

women as principal occupants of the tombs . . . but as a
matter of fact we find fewer women than men. Lastly the
bride chosen for the god would be a virgin, probably
good-looking, certainly young. Shub-ad was a woman of
about forty years of age.[1]

As for the *gigunus* or underground chambers mentioned in
the texts as being near the city gates, Woolley points out that
the ancient wall of the temenos is not contemporary with
the tombs; no relation between the cemetery and the
temenos or between the cemetery and the *ziggurat* terrace
can be shown to exist.

To me the most convincing argument against the "fertility-
rite" theory is that, according to the texts, this rite took place
every year; yet there are only sixteen "royal graves" separated
from each other by a considerable distance of time. Against
this, of course, it might be argued that at infrequent intervals
there were extraordinary rites calling for special ceremonies
and a holocaust of victims; but there is absolutely no written
or archaeological evidence for this.

However, there still remains the question "if these men and
women were indeed kings and queens, why is it that their
names do not appear in the King-Lists?" Yet is this, after all,
so surprising? The names on these Lists purport to be those
of monarchs ruling over the entire land of Sumer. The
cemetery which the Expedition discovered is proved by the
archaeological stratification to have belonged to the period
just before the First Dynasty of Ur. A-bar-gi and Shub-ad
would be local monarchs, or vassals of whatever state then
claimed suzerainty over the entire country, and therefore
would not appear on the King-Lists.

A more difficult problem, as Sir Leonard admits, is that if
"our royal tombs are those of kings accompanied to the grave
by the court which attended them in their lifetime" recognition of this "implies a view of the after-world which neither
the surviving texts nor the evidence of later burial-customs

[1] "Ur Excavations," op. cit.

would warrant our attributing to the Sumerians". For the full appreciation of this and other fascinating problems I must refer the reader to the official publication of the two Museums *Ur Excavations; the Royal Cemeteries* (published by Oxford University Press, 1934) and, for a more summarised Version, to Sir Leonard Woolley's *Excavations at Ur* (Ernest Benn, 1951).

CHAPTER TWELVE

"WELL, OF COURSE, IT'S THE FLOOD..."

OUR knowledge of Sumerian culture has been gradually revealed by scholars of many countries, working on many
sites. At Ur, Woolley and his joint Anglo-American staff
filled in part of the pattern; French archaeologists such as
Henri de Genouillac, Kirshman, Tellier and Parrot, working
at Telloh through twenty campaigns, contributed another
part. The German scholars Jordan, Noldeke, and Heinrich
at Warka, the Englishmen Langdon and Mackay at Jemdet
Nasr, the Americans Schmidt, Lockard, White, Kramer and
others added further information from their excavations at
ancient Shurrupak. Other Americans, under Speiser, dug at
Tepe Gawra. The Oriental Institute of Chicago, the American School of Oriental Research and the Museum of the
University of Philadelphia revealed the wonderful "temple
oval" at Khafajah between 1930–38, besides discovering
many Sumerian statuettes, the Sin Temple, and remains of
private houses. Other archaeologists worked at Medain, Tell
Arpachiyah, Tepe Shenshi, Tell Agrab, Tell Koshi....
Throughout the whole of southern Iraq, between 1920 and
1939, there was a fever of archaeological activity. One by
one, the deserted mounds of crumbling brick, which had
excited Loftus and Churchill during their adventurous
journey nearly a century earlier, were giving up their secrets.

In Professor Pallis's monumental work *The Antiquity of*

Iraq[1] the author devotes 42 pages to a Chronological List of Excavation Sites, detailing the names of these sites, those of the archaeologists who dug them during the past hundred years, and a brief summary of the more important discoveries. A mere handful are quoted in the foregoing paragraph. During the period 1919–1939, according to Professor Pallis's list, no less than thirty-two Mesopotamian sites were being investigated by over one hundred leading archaeologists from Germany, America, Britain, France, Italy and Iraq—and this does not take into account the philologists from these and other countries who, though they did not excavate, assisted their archaeological colleagues from their study desks.

Obviously in a book of this length it is impossible to do justice to the work of every expedition which has worked in Iraq. Even an attempt to summarise the work of half of them would produce only a tedious catalogue of names. Therefore, in directing the reader to the excavations at Ur, I am not suggesting, even by implication, that they have a higher significance than the others; least of all that any one nation, be it British, or German or American, has made the greatest contribution to our knowledge of Sumer. National rivalries occasionally intrude even into archaeology, but on the whole it can proudly claim to be an international science.

It so happens that the work of the Anglo-American expedition at Ur, though confined to only one of the great Sumerian cities, provides a representative sample of several aspects of Sumeriology. It was occupied, more or less continuously, for some four thousand years; its earliest remains dated from the *al 'Ubaid* period to the time of Nebuchadnezzar (605–562 B.C.). There were remains of the *Uruk* and *Jemdet Nasr* cultures, and richly furnished graves dating from a few centuries prior to the First Dynasty of Ur. The skilful technique developed by its excavators, particularly in the preservation of fragile objects of antiquity can stand as a model of scientific archaeology; similar techniques were used, and improved

[1] Copenhagen, Ejner Nunksgaard, Ltd., 1956.

upon, by excavators of other nations working on other sites. Moreover, these archaeologists, such as the Germans at Uruk, and the French at Telloh, were frequently in communication with Woolley, and he with them.

We will take first the question of preservation. Obviously some Sumerian antiquities, such as stone sculpture, clay statuettes and some objects of metal, had as good a chance of survival as those found in, say, Egypt. But a great many others, especially garments, jewellery, and objects such as musical instruments, which were built on a wooden framework, were liable to suffer more than Egyptian antiquities, since they were not in airtight stone chambers in a dry climate, but usually left in direct contact with the corrosive soil. It is this fact which makes more astonishing the state of preservation of such lovely things as the regalia of Queen Shub-ad, her sledge-chariot, her golden goblets and bowls, the "Ram caught in the Thicket" and the ivory-and-lapis panel, with its scenes of war and peace, which Woolley calls "The Standard". Looking at these things as they appear today, resplendent in their gold and semi-precious stones, it is difficult to believe that when found they were mere flattened silhouettes crushed by the weight of forty feet of earth or scattered fragments of inlay only held together by compacted soil, the wooden bases having completely decayed. Yet with infinite skill, patience and care they were restored very nearly to their original appearance.

For example, the lovely harps (or lyres) which were found in the Death Pits were found in a badly crushed and decayed state. In the case of Shub-ad's harp the wooden upright had decayed, but left its impression in the ground. Into this hole plaster of Paris was poured to preserve the shape. The rectangular sound-box had also gone, but much of the mosaic border was intact, and this guaranteed its outline. Strips of shell and lapis-lazuli inlay gave a clue to its decoration; by carefully noting the relative positions of these fragments as found it was possible to reconstruct the whole instrument as it now appears. "In all essentials Shub-ad's harp may be taken as correct. As the oldest example of a harp in existence it is of great interest, not least so because it is of an extremely advanced type."[1] Other instruments found in the death pits were long copper cymbals, silver double-pipes, a drum and a systrum (a sacred rattle used in temple ceremonies).

The extraordinary figure of a goat, of gold and lapis-lazuli standing with forepaws resting on what appears to be a branching bush or tree, is one of two such statues found in the "Great Death-Pit" described in the preceding chapter. "The body had been made of wood over which the gold of head and legs and the silver of the belly had been hammered, and the separate locks of hair carved in shell and lapis-lazuli attached with bitumen".[1] When found the statue had been squashed flat, but had kept its contour. Restoration was a delicate process, involving first the removal of the gold parts from the two flattened sides, which were then secured by waxed muslin, and the two sides cut apart and the inner faces cleaned. "Then waxed muslin was applied to this inner face and it was gradually pressed out until it reproduced the curves of the other broken but uncrushed figure. The gold was annealed and pushed out into shape." It was clearly a ritual object—one recalls the Egyptian "goat-god" Anzety—and had probably stood on an altar. Sir Leonard remarks that it is

> by far the best example yet found of that curious and refined Sumerian art of the goldsmith and lapidary which loved to combine in one object the richest materials and the strongest contrasts of colour and texture, to design in bold lines and to complicate that design with an almost morbid elaboration of detail.

*　　*　　*

Tempting as it is to linger among these lovely and unique relics of the Early Dynastic Period, it is time to return to the main stream of Sumeriological research and consider the other levels into which the Expedition dug at Ur, and the

[1] "Ur Excavations," op. cit.

work of archaeologists working on other Sumerian sites. Apart from the "Royal Cemetery" and the private graves at Ur, perhaps the most dramatic discovery of the Joint Expedition—and the most controversial in its implications— was the so-called "Flood Pit".

Woolley explains how this came to be made.

In the year 1929 the work of excavating the Royal Cemetery at Ur was drawing towards its end. On the evidence then to hand I was convinced that the cemetery came before, but only just before, the First Dynasty of Ur; the treasures recovered from its graves illustrated a civilisation of an astonishingly high order and it was therefore all the more important to trace the steps by which man had reached that level of art and culture. That meant presumably that we had to dig deeper; but it was just as well to begin by a small-scale test of the lower levels which could be carried out with a minimum of time and cost.

Woolley decided to sink a small shaft, not more than five feet square, into the soil which underlay the graves. The workmen dug down through an accumulation of decomposed mud-brick, ashes and pottery fragments for three feet and then, suddenly, every sign of occupation ceased. Only a yard beneath the cemetery the excavators came upon clean water-laid mud. "Virgin soil", said the Arab foreman, and began to make preparations to dig elsewhere. But Woolley was not satisfied; the "virgin soil" was not anything like as deep down as he had expected, so he gave orders to dig deeper. Very reluctantly the foreman agreed and the work continued. Four feet, five feet, six feet . . . and all that the spades threw up was clean mud without a single potsherd or other sign of human occupation. Seven feet, eight feet, nine feet; still nothing. It was not until the excavators had dug some eleven feet below the cemetery, and eight feet below the lowest level of occupation, that, suddenly, there appeared flint implements and painted *al 'Ubaid* pottery.

I got into the pit once more [said Woolley], examined the

sides, and by the time I had written up my notes was quite convinced of what it all meant; but I wanted to see whether others would come to the same conclusion. So I brought up two of my staff, and, pointing out the facts, asked for an explanation. They did not know what to say. My wife came along and was asked the same question, and she turned away, remarking casually, "Well, of course, it's the Flood."

However, one could hardly argue the reality of the Biblical Flood from a pit five yards square. So in 1930 at the beginning of the next season's digging, the Expedition marked out an area some seventy-five feet by sixty in the low ground where the "Royal Cemetery" had been. Here they dug a huge pit which, at the end, reached a depth of no less than sixty-four feet. When it was finished one could have sunk a five-storey building into it. (Though even this was exceeded by the pit which the German excavators dug at Erech.) Before they dug far the ruins of houses were found, built of mud-brick of the "plano-convex" type. Since we shall encounter these bricks at a later stage it will be best to explain their technical significance now. By "plano-convex" the archaeologists mean a brick shaped roughly like a British loaf of bread; i.e. flat along the bottom and sides but curved on top. Why the Sumerians ever decided to use such an awkwardly-shaped building unit is a mystery, but from the beginning of the Dynastic period down to the time of Sargon I (c. 2550 B.C.) it was used throughout Sumer. The *Jemdet Nasr* people used flat-sided bricks, as did the people who came after Sargon I, so obviously any building constructed of these odd-shaped bricks can definitely be dated between these two periods.

Perhaps the briefest and clearest way in which I can illustrate the successive strata which the Expedition found, is to set them out in a column with the most recent layers at the top and the most ancient at the bottom. If one regards this column as the "Flood Pit" this is what Woolley found:

Lower levels of the cemetery

First building stratum. Plano-convex bricks	Eight levels of
Second building stratum. Plano-convex bricks	houses in
Third building stratum. (In lowest levels)	twenty feet.
flat-topped bricks.	

Eighteen feet of broken pottery from a vase-factory. Changes of fashion evident in pottery showed kilns in use for long period.

Upper debris *Jemdet Nasr* ware

Middle debris *Uruk* ware

Heavy disk of baked clay; a potter's wheel used by the *Uruk* people; earliest known example of invention whereby man passed from handcraft to the age of machinery

Al 'Ubaid ware

THE FLOOD

At this point, in Woolley's words "all pottery came to an end and we had . . . the clean silt piled up by the Flood. A few graves had been dug into the silt, and in them was *al 'Ubaid* pottery of a richer sort than in the kiln rubbish above." And there were graves dug in the silt deposit with bodies lying on their backs, rigidly extended, hands crossed below the stomach, a position not found in Mesopotamian graves of any later date until the Greek period. In some of these graves there were terracotta figurines of a type usually found in the ruins of *al 'Ubaid* dwellings.

Then came eleven feet of absolutely clean river silt without a single trace of human or animal occupation. Chemical analysis proved that it was water-laid and composed of material brought down from the middle Euphrates.

Below this eleven-foot layer of mud the Expedition found:

Decayed mud-brick from huts with ashes and potsherds of *al 'Ubaid* pottery of a rich type, in abundance, flints, clay figurines, flat bricks, fragments of clay plaster with the impression of reed-stems.

(a) *Top* Remains of huts set up on belt of mud formed of decayed vegetation.

(b) *Bottom* Stiff green clay with brown stains from weed-roots.

VIRGIN SOIL

"Here," writes Woolley, "we were at the bottom of Mesopotamia."

If we were to judge the development of Sumerian culture only by what was found at Ur, we might conjecture that (*a*) shortly after the first settlers built their reed-and-mud houses on the mudflats of the lower Euphrates, a great catastrophe supervened—the Flood—after which the threads of life were gradually picked up again, and the admixture of new cultures, first the *Uruk* and then the *Jemdet Nasr* peoples, speeded the development of civilisation. Would we be right in this conjecture? We would not.

At Erech (Uruk) at the same time as Sir Leonard Woolley was digging at Ur, German archaeologists found an *al 'Ubaid* stratum forty feet thick—evidence of a long occupation. At Eridu the Iraq Government unearthed fourteen temples one above the other, and all belonged to the period before the Flood. Then why, it might be asked, was there such sparse evidence of pre-Flood occupation at Ur? The answer appears to be that the pit sunk by Woolley and his staff was outside the town, so that the houses discovered represented the city's expansion at a fairly late date. If the pit had been sunk near the centre of Ur the results might have been very different. This evidence alone proves the importance of cross-checking by archaeologists working on different sites.

Again, it might have appeared, from the scanty *al 'Ubaid* remains discovered at Ur below Flood-level, that these people were little better than savages, living at a Neolithic level of culture. Actually, as we know from other excavations, from Persia to the shores of the Mediterranean, they were considerably advanced.

In the house ruins under the Flood silt at Ur we found two beads made of amazonite, a stone of which the nearest known source is the Nilghiri hills of central India; it was a fairly sophisticated community that could import its luxuries from lands far away. . . .[1]

If, now, we combine the archaeological evidence with that provided by the written documents, what do we see? As described in Chapter Nine, a vigorous mountain people from the highlands of Iran, with a long cultural tradition, establish themselves first in northern Iraq and later—as the Gulf recedes—on the newborn islands of the lower Euphrates. Suddenly there is a catastrophe of such magnitude that it imprints itself indelibly on the minds of the survivors—the Deluge. We know that even today the Euphrates and Tigris rivers are subject to sudden and violent flooding. After a period of exceptionally heavy rain in the northern mountains, millions of tons of water sweep down on to the flat southern plain. The embankments give way, and the rivers burst out, spreading from horizon to horizon, leaving only a few isolated "Tells" or mounds rising above a waste of waters. Such a catastrophe must have occurred during the al 'Ubaid period, some six thousand years ago.

> Eleven feet of silt [writes Woolley] would probably mean a flood not less than twenty-five feet deep; in the flat low-lying land of Mesopotamia a flood of that depth would cover an area about three hundred miles wide and a hundred miles across; the whole of the fertile land between the Elmaite (Persian) mountains would disappear, every village would be destroyed, and only a few of the old cities, set high on their built-up mounds, would survive the disaster.

To the al 'Ubaid people of southern Mesopotamia such an event would mark the end of the world as they knew it. And among the few who survived there would be writers who were moved to record the event in imperishable epic verse, which, preserved and elaborated by the much later Hebrew poets, has passed into our own sacred canon. Centuries after the Great Flood a Sumerian poet, repeating an oral tradition of his ancestors, could write:

[1] *Excavations at Ur,* op. cit.

Consternation over Adad reaches to the heavens,
Turning to blackness all that has been light.
(The wide) land is shattered like (a pot)
For one day the south-storm (blew)
Gathering speed as it blew (submerging the mountains)
Overtaking the people like a battle.
No-one can see his fellow,
Nor can the people be from heaven. . . .[1]

And a much later Hebrew poet, borrowing from the Sumerian tradition, wrote in Genesis:

... the same day were all the fountains of the great deep broken up, and the windows of heaven were opened. And the rain was upon the earth forty days and forty nights. . . . And the waters prevailed, and were increased greatly upon the earth. . . . And all flesh died that moved upon the earth, both fowl, and of cattle, and of beast, and of every creeping thing that creepeth upon the earth, and every man. All in whose nostrils was the breath of life, of all that was in the dry land, died. . . .

Millions perished but a small number survived. One such man, in the Sumerian poem named Utnapishtim, took wise precautions, and under the command of God built himself a ship:

Man of Shurrupak, son of Ubar-Tutu,
Tear down this house, build a ship!
Give up possessions, and seek thou life!
Despise property and keep the soul alive!
Aboard the ship take thou the seed of living things.
The ship that thou shalt build
Her dimensions shall be to measure.
Equal shall be her width and her length.
Like the Apsu shalt thou seal her. . . .

This was the poem, part of which Goerge Smith deciphered in the British Museum. And surely this same poem

[1] *Ancient Near Eastern Texts*, Princeton University Press, 1950. (Translation of *The Epic of Gilgamesh* by E. A. Speiser.)

must have been known to the author of Genesis when he
wrote:

> Make thee an ark of gopher wood; rooms shall thou make
> in the ark, and shalt pitch it within and without with
> pitch.[1] And this is the fashion which thou shalt make it of;
> the length of the ark shall be three hundred cubits, the
> breadth of it fifty cubits, and the height of it thirty cubits.
> . . . And, behold I, even I, do bring a flood of waters upon
> the earth, to destroy all flesh, wherein is the breath of life,
> from under heaven; and everything that is in the earth
> shall die.

The new scientific generation of archaeologists is usually
embarrassed by any attempt to present the romantic aspect
of their vocation. In some ways they are probably right;
lush "popularisation", the selective emphasis of "buried
treasure" may tend to give a false picture of what to them is
essentially cool scientific research, like nuclear physics. Well,
let them blush, for surely the story I have to tell in this
chapter is capable of stirring even the least imaginative man
or woman.

It is a story which penetrates to the very roots of our culture and religion. One hundred years ago Layard and
Botta find, in the destroyed palace of an Assyrian king,
thousands of baked-clay tablets. Twenty years later an obscure bank-note engraver named Smith notices, among these
tablets, one which purports to tell the story of a Deluge
which destroyed mankind. A London newspaper sends him
out to Iraq to find the vital missing fragment of the tablet.
He does so, and shortly afterwards dies. Sixty years pass,
and then a group of men and women, hundreds of miles
south of Kuyujnik, where Smith discovered the missing piece
of baked clay, find themselves staring at a layer of water-
laid mud deep beneath the ruins of a Sumerian city. And
one of them says, casually, "Well, of course, it's the
Flood. . . ."

[1] I.e. bitumen, which is abundant in Iraq.

CHAPTER THIRTEEN

PORTRAIT OF SUMER

BUT was it *the* Deluge? Some archaeologists, for instance Mr. Seton Lloyd, think not. They argue that the eight-foot stratum of mud which Woolley found was not necessarily evidence of the Biblical flood, but one flood among many. They point out that when a second pit was sunk in the central part of Ur, no mud-stratum was found, though Sir Leonard explains this by suggesting that the earliest settlement at Ur was placed on a little hill out of reach of the Flood, and it was this hill into which the second pit was sunk. This seems to me a reasonable explanation, but it does not satisfy Mr. Lloyd. "Traces of similar floods", he says, "appear upon other sites, often at an entirely different period in their history, and it is doubtful if any of these may rightly be called *the* Flood."[1]

I regard these arguments as irrelevant. Obviously there must have been, at a very early period in Sumerian history, a deluge of such magnitude and destructive power that it practically blotted out all life. The "King-List" specifically states:

The Flood came. After the Flood came, kingship again was sent down from on high.

In other words, civilisation was temporarily destroyed, and when it was restored a new dynasty of kings ruled the

[1] Lloyd, Seton. *Mesopotamia*, Lovat Dickson, 1936.

country. To me this discussion has a somewhat sinister contemporaneity. If a thousand or two thousand years hence, future archaeologists dig down into the submerged strata of London, or New York, or Moscow, they may find evidence of an atomic blast which destroyed life. Below that strata they might find remains of television sets, juke-boxes, refrigerators, cinemas and other relics of our materialistic civilisation. Above the layer of destruction they may find evidences of a new and different kind of civilisation, perhaps non-European. They might argue about the date of the catastrophe, but there could be no doubt about its reality.

Similarly, in ancient Sumer there must have been, among many destructive floods, one which imprinted itself on the memory of mankind, so that it became the subject of epic verse, and was even absorbed into the religious literature of other, later peoples, such as the Assyrians and the Hebrews. The similarities between the story of Utnapishtim and Noah are too great to be accidental. And here I must express respectful disagreement with Mr. D. J. Wiseman, who, in his book *Illustrations from Biblical Archaeology*[1] says:

> The differences between this epic (the Babylonian account of Creation) and the Hebrew accounts... are too numerous for the Genesis story to have evolved from the Babylonian. Any similarities with the Genesis record have to be overlaying extraneous matter which forms the bulk of the poem; such can best be explained as due to both versions going back to a common primary fact.

Exactly. And the "common primary fact" is a colossal deluge which practically destroyed lower Mesopotamia some six thousand or more years ago. Both the archaeological and the documentary evidence are there, staring us in the face. Whether or not Woolley's "Flood-pit" represents the sediment left by the Great Flood or another one is immaterial.

[1] Wiseman, D. J. *Illustrations from Biblical Archaeology*, Tyndale Press, 1959.

The fact remains that there *was* a great flood. And it happened in lower Mesopotamia, in the "Land of Shinar".

* * *

During and after the Second World War further excavations of Sumerian sites were carried out, and some are still in progress. The Iraq Government's Department of Antiquities played an increasingly important part in these activities, and the Baghdad Museum now contains one of the largest collections of Sumerian and Babylonian antiquities in the world. Among its most important digs was the one at Tell Hasuna, under the direction of Seton Lloyd and Fuad Safar, where six levels of occupation were discovered, *all pre-al 'Ubaid*. Muhammed Al Mustafa dug at Tell al Dhiba'i, unearthing five strata from Akkadian to Kassite times.

Chicago's Oriental Institute in collaboration with the American School of Oriental Research, Baghdad, dug several important sites from 1948 onwards, examining prehistoric sites at Matarrah, Kal'at Jarmo, Barda Balka, and the Greater Zab River Drainage Basin. The archaeologists concerned, among whom were Robert J. Braidwood, Linda Braidwood, Bruce Howe and H. E. Wright, Junr., concentrated mainly on the lower, neolithic levels, excavating village sites and prehistoric caves, reaching back to the earliest appearance of Man in Mesopotamia. Meanwhile, some of the more familiar sites were re-examined; *Nimrud* by Mr. E. L. Mallowan (British School of Archaeology), *Assur* by the German scholars Preusser and Haller (Deutsche Orient-Gesellshaft, Berlin), *Uruk* by H. Lenzen (also of the Deutsche Orient-Gesellshaft) and *Nippur* by McCown, Steele and Kramer (University of Pennsylvania).

As a result of the devoted work of three generations of archaeologists and explorers, from the time of Claudius Rich down to the present day, we now know a great deal about the Sumerians; about their origins, their language, their religion and social customs; about how they looked, how they dressed, about their agriculture, their methods of trade, legal and administrative systems, and their imaginative literature. The story is not—and probably never will be—complete, but sufficient material is available at least to attempt a profile.

We have already dealt very briefly with Sumerian origins in Chapter Ten. In Chapters Eleven to Thirteen we have seen what one Sumerian city—Ur of the Chaldees—could produce at the dawn of the Dynastic Period (c. 2700 B.C.). What happened afterwards?

Intelligible written records begin at about 3000 B.C. From these, and from archaeological research, it is evident that even at this early period there were large cities with splendid temples and elaborately-planned houses. Stone-carving was well-developed, also metal-working and the fashioning of jewellery. Extensive foreign trade contributed lapis-lazuli from Afghanistan, shells from the Persian Gulf and rare stones such as calcite, obsidian and diorite, none of which are found in southern Mesopotamia. But in the early Dynastic Period there was no unified state of Sumer, unlike Egypt which had become unified by 3200 B.C.

In Sumer by 3000 B.C. or earlier, civilisation had followed a different course. While there was no centralised state system under one monarch, strong independent city-states were in existence. Eridu, Ur, Erech, Umma, Larsa, Kissura, Adab, Nippur . . . each had developed a high degree of civic organisation; each had its cluster of farms and orchards watered by well-planned irrigation canals; each had its local monarch or governor, its elaborate temples and priesthood. For instance Ur, which today is a mere waste of sun-dried brick many miles from the nearest river, was once a mighty port. The head of the Persian Gulf, which is now some eighty miles to the south, then came almost to the ramparts of the city, and quays ran deep into the maze of narrow streets.

Most of the houses within the walled enclosure were almost exactly like those in which the Iraqi peasants live today; small-roomed, mud-brick dwellings with flat roofs; the system of agriculture, the crops grown, the food eaten, and the cattle raised, were much the same in ancient Sumer as in 1957. The main difference was in public buildings, the palaces of the kings and the high-walled temples and towers.[1]

It has been estimated that, at the height of its expansion, half a million people lived within the four square miles of Ur —somewhat more than the population of Brunswick, in modern Germany, or Indianapolis, in the United States. Such cities as Kish, Nippur, Eridu and Lagash, had comparable populations.

In considering the historical period during which these cities flourished, the reader must bear one very important fact in mind, especially when comparing the "King-Lists" of Sumer with those of Ancient Egypt. The Egyptian "King-Lists" cover a period of nearly *three thousand years*. The Sumerian lists, impressive though they appear, probably extend over seven hundred at the most. The reason is that many of these Dynastic lists are not consecutive as are those of Egypt, but record the names of monarchs who were reigning from different cities *at the same time*.

Considering the palpable absurdity of the lengths of reign credited to the earliest Sumerian kings (241,200 years) can any reliance be placed on the Lists? At one time scholars tended to dismiss them as mythical fabrications, but not now. Even the kings who reigned before the Flood may have been real enough, though in process of time they have become shadowy figures, half-gods, half-men. But after the Flood, when as the records tell us "kingship was again sent down from on high", the reigns become of normal human length, and the monuments of such kings as A-anni-pad-da King of Ur, son of Mes-anni-pad-da King of Ur, have been discovered. In the same city contemporary records were found of the great Sargon of Akkad, including a portrait-group of his daughter, who was High Priestess of the Moon God.

At other Sumerian sites the records and monuments of

[1] Cottrell, Leonard. *Lost Cities*, Robert Hale, 1957.

other Kings and Governors have been discovered, which establish them as real people; Enannatum I and Entemena at Lagash, Sargon and Naram-Sin at Agade (Akkad), Lugal-Zaggisi and Dumuzi at Uruk, Ur-Nammu and Dungi at Ur, are a few examples.

Any attempt to establish a positive chronology of this historical period is hazardous. For example, when Woolley found at al 'Ubaid the tablet of A-anni-pad-da, Assyriologists estimated that the First Dynasty of Ur (which the Royal Cemetery preceded) started at about 3100 B.C., and he accordingly gave this date in his publication *Ur Excavations*. But not long after the book was published in 1934 a revised chronology was introduced which brought the date of the First Dynasty down to 2900 B.C. In recent years some scholars have preferred to date it even later, to 2700 B.C., roughly contemporary with the building of the Great Pyramid in Egypt.

If, therefore, we accept *c.* 2700 B.C. as the beginning of the First Dynasty of Ur, and *c.* 2000 B.C. as marking the end of Sumerian civilisation, the Dynastic or "historical" period covers, at the most, seven centuries.

Yet what an achievement those centuries mark! Constantly hampered by inter-city rivalries, by unprotected frontiers across which envious barbarians moved down to harry and plunder, still the Sumerians succeeded in protecting, developing and maintaining their high civilisation; and not only protecting it but at times extending it by force of arms to neighbouring countries. Sargon I of Akkad is believed to have pushed his conquests as far as the Mediterranean coast. It is not surprising that the Sumerians rarely achieved complete unity, such as Egypt with her almost inviolable frontiers enjoyed. Yet perhaps, as with the Greeks some two thousand years later, the rivalry between Sumerian city-states provided a sharp, competitive impetus which was lacking in the more settled civilisation of the Nile.

Who the Sumerians were, how they originated, is still largely a mystery, in spite of the archaeologists' endeavours

to trace their origins to the mountains of Persia and central
Turkey. One fact is certain; they were not Semitic. Most probably, as we have seen in Chapter Nine, the culture which
was called Sumerian was a mixture of several strains, *Tell
Halaf, Al 'Ubaid, Uruk, Jemdet Nasr* . . . but these are mere
archaeological labels concealing the identities of peoples so
remote from us in time that they can only be studied by their
pottery, tools, weapons and other artefacts.

With the invention of writing, which was developed by the
Jemdet Nasr people and came to full fruition in the Dynastic
Period, the Sumerians become articulate. We no longer
know them only through their objects found in their ruined
cities; they can speak to us directly. In 2500 B.C. they are
living in large, highly organised cities surrounded by farms
and orchards which they have won from the fertile mud of
the Tigris–Euphrates valleys. Where once their ancestors
lived in reed-and-mut huts on islands reclaimed from the
swamps there is now a complex system of irrigation canals
and ditches, carrying water from the rivers many miles inland.

First one sees the dusty, wide-spreading plain, stretching
without interruption on either side of the rivers until it
merges with the sky. On each side of the broad muddy
rivers are green fields of wheat, barley, and other cereals,
threaded by canals and ditches. There are date-palms,
olive-groves and plantations and figs and vines.

Some land is given over to pasture, grazed by sheep,
goats, and cattle in large numbers. It is an orderly landscape, in which the land is carefully divided and appor-
tioned; much is owned by the god and the priesthoods
who serve him, other land is owned by the king and his
officers.[1]

In the primitive communities which exist today in Asia,
Africa and Latin America, the produce of the soil is barely
sufficient to maintain the people who live on and from it.

[1] Cottrell, Leonard. *The Anvil of Civilisation*, Faber & Faber, 1958.

The only visible manifestations of communal living are the African *kraal* or the *adobe* huts of a Mexican village. Civilisation can only exist when there is surplus wealth. Look again at the Sumerian landscape. Above and beyond the sweating backs of the peasants working in the fields, or knee-deep in the muddy canals, we see the city. First, the outer suburbs mingling with the fields; then a high defensive wall, within which are thousands of mud-brick dwellings, each with its tiny courtyard and doorways opening on to a network of narrow streets. Higher still another great rampart breaks the skyline, the outer wall of the Temple Enclosure, the home of the God who rules the city. But it is really much more than that. It is also the centre of civic administration and higher education—Town Hall, University and Cathedral in one. Soaring into the intense blue sky, even higher than the Temple itself, rises a huge tiered tower, like a medieval castle-keep. This is the *ziggurat*, made of mud-brick reinforced and ornamented with millions of brilliantly-coloured fragments of pottery.[1] A flight of steps leads to the summit, where an asphalt platform supports a temple with white washed walls and many dark, narrow chambers. In one of these rooms lives the God or Goddess of the city, before whom incense burns perpetually.

Not one of the farm labourers working in the fields outside the city will ever penetrate this chamber. Among the thousands of priests who throng the Temple only a few, of the highest rank, will be privileged to enter the presence of the Deity. Yet every man and woman, from King, Queen, Governor and High Priest, down to the lowliest labourer in the far-spreading farms beyond the city walls, believes that the preservation of his life, the fertility of his land, and its protection from flood, drought and enemy attack, rest in the hands of the guardian God or Goddess. It might be Anu, god of the sky, Ki, the earth-goddess, Enlil, war-leader and storm-god, or Enki, god of the waters. In every case it is the

[1] A similar kind of colourful encrustation is used in the Buddhist temples of Siam today. L.C.

God who rules the city, and all, including the monarch himself, give Him precedence.

*   *   *

The rivers swarm with craft, from small fishing-boats to large transports and the luxurious vessels of the rich, each with its upswept prow and stern, its enclosed cabin and sun-awnings. In the fields the harvesters swing their sickles; along the dusty roads move trains of pack-animals, ox-drawn wagons carrying farm produce, four-wheeled war-chariots drawn by asses (the horse has not yet appeared in Mesopotamia) and ranks of bronze-helmeted infantry, marching smartly in step.

Everywhere—in contrast to the same scene today—there is *colour*, and a hard, bright glitter. There is colour in the lush variegated green of the fields, laced by the sun-reflecting canals, and in the gem-like flowers which the Sumerian jewellers copied so lovingly in the head-dress of Queen Shub-ad and her ladies. There is colour in the dress of both men and women; scarlet and orange and yellow garments contrast with the sun-browned skins of their wearers. The men naked to the waist, apart from ornaments; the women of the higher classes wear long, loose-fitting gowns[1] which leave one shoulder bare. Their hair is dark—the Sumerians were known among themselves as "the black-headed people" —and many wear wigs relieved by brightly-coloured ornaments. The more sophisticated women emphasise their charms with cosmetics such as lip-rouge and eye-shadow. They oil and perfume their bodies and the wealthier among them wear much jewellery. Many of the men are bearded, though the priests are clean-shaven. But in general appearance the Sumerians are somewhat less attractive to European taste than the slimmer, more elegant Ancient Egyptians; they tend to be short and stocky, with a tendency to run to

[1] This description applies mainly to the Sumerian summer scene. In winter, and during the cold Mesopotamian nights, they wore heavier garments, often of sheep or other animal skins, and cloaks were worn.

fat in middle age. Often the older men have a portly, alder-
manic look, with pot-bellies, prominent noses and eyes.

Entering the main gate of the city which pierces the pon-
derous wall, we are soon lost in a maze of narrow streets,
thronged with people and traffic. Naked children play near
the open doorways, from which comes the clang of hammers
on metal, the grunt of saws, the whirring of potters' wheels.
This is the artisans' quarter. Sometimes the clatter of a
military chariot drowns other sounds, as the heavy, solid
wheeled vehicle with its helmeted driver and spearman,
thunders along the street, sending men, women and children
scurrying for safety. Ripe Sumerian curses follow it.

Higher still we enter a richer, somewhat quieter area,
where the houses are larger, though the small, narrow windows fronting the streets afford no indication of the beauty
and elegance within.

These are the homes of the rich merchants and the higher
officials of the Court. Glance through one of the window-
grills (there is no glass, only bars of mud-brick) and we see a
dinner-party in progress. The guests are seated on backless
chairs, beside light tables of wood or reed wickerwork. The
food includes garlic in sour cream, milk and barley soup,
roast Tigris salmon and roast pig. The dessert comprises
various fruit such as dates, pomegranates, and figs, and there
is an excellent goat's milk cheese. To accompany the feast
there is an abundance of wine, for the vine—the inevitable
accompaniment of true civilisation—is grown in Sumer as it
was in Egypt, Persia, Greece and Rome. For those who pre-
fer it there is also beer, which is usually drunk through a
straw.

The girls are "lashed-up" to the eyes. Heavy discs of gold
dangle on soft brown shoulders, and the lustrous black wigs,
framing the dark, deep-shadowed eyes, are adorned with
gold "beech-leaf" pendants overhanging the brow. Crowning
the wigs are intertwined strings of blue and red beads, from
which spring delicate artificial flowers made from lapis-
lazuli and gold. The women drink with the men, from fluted

goblets of gold and silver, while in the background musicians play for the dance or provide a thrumming accompaniment to the impassioned recital of some old Sumerian poem. It might be, perhaps, the epic of Gilgamesh and of how he fought the storm-god and won the love of the goddess Inanna; it might be the story of the Great Flood, and of Utnapishtim, who built himself an Ark which was borne up on the waters which destroyed the world.

Perhaps some guest calls for the story which relates how the goddess Ninmu was wooed by the god Enki:

> *The Goddess Ninmu came out to the river bank,*
> *Enki in the marshlands looks about, looks about.*
> *He says to his messenger, Isimud,*
> *"Shall I not kiss Ninmu, the fair?"*
> *His messenger Isimud answers*
> *"Kiss the young one, the fair,*
> *Kiss Ninmu, the fair,*
> *For my king I shall blow up a mighty wind"*
>
> *Alone he sets food in the boat,*
> *A second time he set there. . . .*
> *He embraced her, he kissed her,*
> *Enki poured the seed into the womb,*
> *She took the seed into the womb, the seed of Enki,*
> *One day being her one month,*
> *Two days being her two months,*
> *Nine days being her nine months, the months of*
> *"womanhood"*
> *Like . . . cream, like . . . cream, like good, princely*
>   *cream*
> *Ninmu, like . . . cream. like . . . cream, like good*
>   *princely cream,*
> *Gave birth to the goddess Ninkurra . . ."*

The goddess, it will be noted, gives birth to her daughter Ninkurra painlessly, in nine days; nor is this surprising, since it took place in Dilmun, the Sumerian Paradise. And, as Professor Kramer suggests in his book *History Begins at Sumer*,

> There is good indication that the Biblical paradise, which is described as a garden planted *eastwards* of Eden, from whose waters flow the four world rivers including the Tigris and Euphrates, may have been originally identical with Dilmun, the Sumerian paradise-land.[1]

*   *   *

A high moon silvers the walls of the sleeping city, and throws deep shadows in the canyons of its streets. Here and there people are still awake; there is shrill laughter from the taverns and brothels. Somewhere a smith's forge sends out a rosy glow, or a fire burns far out across the sleeping fields. But the guests have called for their litters and gone home. The servants have put out the lamps, and the musicians departed with their instruments. Occasionally the thin bray of a trumpet, or a shouted word of command, reminds us that the watchers of the city are still on guard. Otherwise all is silent. But as we stumble back through the dark, unlighted streets to our lodging, we may occasionally look back. And there, glimpsed at the end of a deserted street, or reared high above a huddle of mean dwellings, rises the *ziggurat*. Bathed in moonlight, serene and still, the mighty mass dominates the city as a castle or cathedral lours above the sleeping streets of Rheims or Carcasonne. There, unsleeping, lives the God on whose beneficence the lives and prosperity of everyone, from peasant to monarch, ultimately depend.

[1] Kramer, S. N. *History Begins at Sumer*, Thames & Hudson, 1958.

CHAPTER FOURTEEN

SUMERIAN LAW

ONE of the earliest known Sumerian documents which can be said truly to embody a legal code is the so-called "Lipit-Ishtar Lawcode". In its existing form—which is not complete—it is inscribed on seven baked-clay tablets, six of which were found at Nippur by the American expedition, and the seventh, of unknown provenance, is in the Paris Louvre. Of these tablets four are merely excerpts from the complete code, which has not yet been discovered. The remaining three are fragments of a large, probably twenty-column tablet which had originally contained the entire code of laws. One can only hope that some day the rest of the code will come to light. However, sufficient remains to give us a sketchy idea of Sumerian law in the first half of the second millennium B.C.

Like the much later Code of Hammurabi, the "Lipit-Ishtar Lawcode" consists of (a) a prologue, (b) the legal text and (c) an epilogue. It gets its name from a king named Lipit-Ishtar, fifth ruler of the Dynasty of Isin. The prologue begins with a statement by this king that, after the gods Anu and Enlil had given to the goddess Ninisinna a favourable reign in her city Isin, they had called him, Lipit-Ishtar, to rule the land. He then goes on to tell us of the various reforms he introduced into his kingdom in order to safeguard the welfare of his people:

> ... to establish justice in the land, to banish complaints, to turn back enmity and rebellion ... and to bring

well-being to the Sumerians and Akkadians, then I, Lipit-
Ishtar, the humble shepherd of Nippur, the stalwart
farmer of Erech . . . established justice in Sumer and
Akkad in accordance with the word of Enlil . . . I made
the father support his children (and) I made the children
(support their) father; I made the father (stand) by his
children and (I) made the father (stand by) their
father. . . .

Then comes the most interesting part of the document, a
code of laws, of which the following are a few representative
extracts.

If a man gave bare ground to (another) man to set out an
orchard (and the latter) did not complete setting out that
bare ground as an orchard, he shall give to the man who
set out the orchard the bare ground which he neglected, as
part of his share.

If a man cut down a tree in the garden of (another) man,
he shall pay one-half mina of silver.

If adjacent to the house of a man the bare ground of (another) man has been neglected and the owner of the house
has said to the owner of the bare ground "Because your
ground has been neglected someone may break into my
house; strengthen your house" (and) this agreement has
been confirmed by him, the owner of the bare ground shall
restore to the owner of the house any property that is lost.

If a slave-girl or slave of a man has fled into the heart of the
city (and) *it has been confirmed* that he (or she) dwelt in the
house of (another) man for one month, he shall give slave
for slave.

. . . If the master of an estate or the mistress of an estate has
defaulted on the tax of the estate (and) a stranger has
borne it, for three years he (the owner) may not be evicted.
(Afterwards) the man who bore the tax of the estate shall
possess that estate and the (former) owner of the estate
shall not raise any claim.

If a man's wife has not borne him children (but) a harlot (from) the public square has borne him children, he shall provide grain, oil and clothing for that harlot; the children which the harlot has borne him shall be his heirs, and as long as his wife lives the harlot shall not live in the house with his wife.

If a man has turned his face away from his *first* wife . . . (but) she has not gone out of the (house) his wife which he married *as his favourite* is a second wife; he shall continue to support his first wife.[1]

These are only a few of the thirty-eight laws comprising the code, but many are in an incomplete condition and cannot be understood. Nevertheless those that remain show a rough and ready sense of justice and "fair play". All are essentially practical, and are obviously based on concrete cases; e.g. "If a man rented an ox (and) damaged its eye, he shall pay one half of (its) price" and "If a man rented an ox and broke its horn, he shall pay one fourth of (its) price." "Fair enough," one might comment; but there is nothing in this so-called Code of Laws which suggests a body of jurisprudence, an abstract conception of "the law" administered by a judiciary trained in its precepts. The Lipit-Ishtar Lawcode is, in fact, just the kind of rough and ready set of rules which one might expect to find among an agricultural and pastoral community. One suspects that as new cases came up for judgement, and decisions were reached by the magistrates, the results were added to the code as a precedent, and that was that.

Another interesting legal document was discovered at a place called Abu Harmal, which once formed part of the kingdom of Eshnunna, near modern Baghdad. The city of Eshnunna was located at Tell Asmar, and was excavated by the Oriental Institute of the University of Chicago. The texts, written on fifteen tablets, were found at Tell Abu

[1] Translated by S. N. Kramer. *Ancient Near Eastern Texts*, Princeton University Press, 1955, p. 159.

Harmal by the Iraq Directorate of Antiquities. Like the older Lipit-Ishtar Lawcode it is essentially down-to-earth and practical. Here are a few specimen laws.

If a boatman is negligent and causes the sinking of the boat, he shall pay in full everything the sinking of which he caused. . . .

The hire of a donkey is 1 *seah* of barley, and the wages for its driver are 1 *seah* of barley. He shall drive it the whole day.

The wages of a hired man are 1 shekel of silver; his provender is 1 pan of barley. He shall work for one month.

Should the son of a man bring bride-money to the house of (his) father-in-law, if one of the two deceases, the money shall revert to its owner.

If he takes her (the girl) and she enters his house, but *afterwards* the young woman shall decease, he (the husband) cannot obtain refunded that which he brought (to his father-in-law) but will retain the excess (in) his (hand).

There is one clause in this code which reminds one strongly of the Biblical story of Ruth.

If a man calls at the house of (his) father-in-law, and his father-in-law *accepts* him *in servitude*, but (nevertheless) gives his daughter to (another man) the father of the girl shall refund the bride-money which he received twofold.

Another clause recalls only too vividly the plight of the man who is long away at the wars and returns to find his wife has remarried.

If a man has been made prisoner during a raid or an invasion or (if) he has been carried off forcibly and (stayed in) a foreign country for a (long) time (and if) another man has taken his wife and she has borne him a son—when he returns he shall (get) his wife back.

Property deals are mentioned. Here is one particularly humane law which has no parallel today.

If a man is hard up and sells his house, the owner of the house shall (be entitled to) redeem (it) whenever the purchaser (re)sells it.

Nor is the following extraordinary law likely to be found in any modern legal code.

If a man bites the nose of a(nother) man and severs it, he shall pay 1 mina of silver. (For) an eye (he shall pay) 1 mina of silver; (for) a tooth $\frac{1}{2}$ mina; (for) an ear $\frac{1}{2}$ mina; (for) a slap in the face 10 shekels of silver.

And—

If a man hits another man *accidentally* he shall pay 10 shekels of silver.

On the whole the Code of Eshnunna seems wise and humane, and contains some articles which might well be copied today. This one for instance:

If a wall is threatening to fall and the authorities have brought the fact to the knowledge of the owner (if nevertheless) he does not strengthen his wall, the wall collapses and causes a free man's death, then it is a capital offence; jurisdiction of the king.[1]

Among other Sumerian documents there is a report of a trial of one "Nana-sig, Lu-Ianna" and others alleged to have "killed Lu-Inanna, the son of Lugal-apindu". The dead man's wife, Nin-dada, brought the matter before the court, which consisted of the King (or Governor) of Isin, Ur-Ninurta, and the Assembly of Nippur.

Various witnesses come forward to testify to the killing; "Ur-gula, son of Lugal . . . Dudu, the bird-hunter, Ali-ellati, the dependent, Buzu, the son of Lu-Sin . . . Lugal-Kan the gardener," etc., and boldly state to the Assembly—

[1] Translated Albrecht Goetze. *Ancient Near Eastern Texts*, op. cit., pp. 161–163.

They who have killed a man are not worthy of life. Those three males and that woman should be killed in front of the chair of Lu-Inanna, the son of Lugal-apindu. . . .

The interesting fact out of this case is that it is the first known example of a legal precedent. One might call it "the case of the silent wife". For, as the record states, the unfortunate man's wife, Nin-dada, "opened not her mouth; her lips remained sealed". And the accusers, nine in all, proposed that not only the actual murderers but the wife of the dead man should all be executed, since the wife's silence argued complicity in the murder.

The reply of the august Assembly of Nippur is memorable and the fact that this document was copied several times suggests that it established a precedent in law. This is what the Assembly said:

A woman whose husband did not support her—granted that she knew her husband's enemies, and that (after) her husband had been killed she heard that her husband had been killed—why should she not remain silent about him? Is it (she?) who killed her husband. The punishment of those who actually killed should suffice.

In other words, the judges did not regard Nin-dada as "an accessory after the fact". In this, as Professor Kramer points out, the Sumerian magistrates took the same view as would a modern western court; for a person to be accessory to a crime, that person must "not only know that the felony was committed, but must also receive, relieve, comfort or assist the felon".[1]

Judgement was given against the nine men, who were sentenced to execution, but Nin-dada was discharged, free of guilt. One cannot judge the Sumerian legal system by this one isolated example, but if typical it suggests that this was based on a humane and civilised code of conduct. There are, however, other laws which suggest the opposite, particularly in the Code of Hammurabi. This famous Code, though later

[1] Kramer, S. N. *History Begins at Sumer*, op. cit., pp. 97–98.

than any of the aforementioned examples, contains elements
of Sumerian law which had been handed down to Babylonian times. It is much more comprehensive than the former
codes, and in some ways shows a more modern sense of
justice. It contains regulations governing such questions of
responsibility for (or exemption from) military service; control of trade in alcoholic drinks; security of tenure; the responsibility of a man towards his wife and children, and the
responsibility of a husband to pay his wife's debts. Curiously
it is more harsh towards upper-class offenders than against
the poor committing the same offence. The death penalty was
imposed not only for homicide, but for theft, adultery, and
bearing false witness. Women's rights were closely safe-
guarded. A neglected wife could obtain a divorce "on condition that she had always led a blameless life". Even a con-
cubine who had become a mother was entitled to restitution
of whatever she brought with her to her master's house.

Hammurabi was the sixth of eleven kings of the Old Babylonian (Amorite) Dynasty. He ruled for forty-three years,
from 1728 to 1686 B.C., and was famous as a just and beneficent ruler and a mighty lawgiver. The *stele* (inscribed stone
tablet) on which the code is written was discovered in the
winter of 1901–1902 by French archaeologists working at
Susa (the Shushan of Esther and Daniel). This was the capital
of the Elamites, and the *stele* had evidently been carried there
as a trophy of war by some Elamite ruler after a successful
raid on Babylonia. For some obscure reason the Elamites had
chipped off certain of the laws, but fortunately these have
been preserved in other copies of the Code. This great document, the oldest legal code in the world, has been translated
by several scholars, from 1902 onwards. The translation from
which the following extracts were taken is by Theopile J.
Meek in that excellent compendium of Near Eastern writings
Ancient Near Eastern Texts Relating to the Old Testament edited
by James B. Pritchard and published, in 1955, by the Princeton University Press.

There are 282 clauses in the Code, in addition to the

Prologue in which the king tells us how he was named by the god Enlil:

> . . . to promote the welfare of the people, me, Hammurabi, the devout, god-fearing prince, to cause justice to prevail in the land, to destroy the wicked and the evil. That the strong might not oppress the weak. . . .

These were noble aims, but it seems to the present writer that Hammurabi's wisdom and justice are sometimes overpraised by those who are overawed by the great age of his Code. It is true that it does contain a number of sensible and practical laws concerning property, land, inheritance, marriage and divorce, but the penalties imposed for criminal offences are extremely harsh, though perhaps not more than those enacted in Britain and other European countries 150 years ago.

As one would expect in an agricultural economy, many of these enactments deal with the cultivation, maintenance, yield and tenure of land. Here are a few examples:

> If a seignior[1] rented a field for cultivation, but has not produced grain in the field, they shall prove that he did no work in the field and he shall give grain to the owners of the field on the basis of those adjoining it. . . . If he did not cultivate the field, but has neglected it, he shall give grain to the owner of the field on the basis of those adjoining it; furthermore the field which he has neglected he shall break up with mattocks, harrow and return to the owner of the field.

> If a seignior rented a fallow field for three years for development, but became so lazy that he has not developed the field, in the fourth year he shall break up the field with mattocks, plough and harrow it, and he shall return (it) to the owner of the field. . . .

---

[1] This word *aivelum*, means literally "man" but in a legal sense it often meant "nobleman" or "free man".

Allowances are made, however, for natural catastrophes.

If a seignior let his field to a tenant, and has already received the rent of the field, (and) later Adad (the storm god) has inundated his field or a flood has ravaged it, the loss shall be the tenant's.

and—

If a debt is outstanding against a seignior and Adad has inundated his field or a flood has ravaged (it) or through lack of water grain has not been produced in the field he shall not make any return of grain to his creditor in that year; he shall cancel his contract-tablet and he shall pay no interest for that year.

Many of the laws relate to the lending and borrowing of money. Interest rates are set, and there are penalties for charging higher interest.

If a merchant (lent) grain at interest, he shall receive sixty *qu* of grain per *kur* as interest. If he lent money at interest, he shall receive one sixth (shekel) six *se* (i.e. one-fifth shekel) per shekel of silver as interest.

If a merchant lent grain or money at interest and when he lent (it) at interest he paid out the money by the small weight and the grain by the small measure, but when he got (it) back he got the money by the (large) weight (and) the grain by the large measure, that merchant shall forfeit whatever he lent.

Builders and contractors in ancient Sumer would have envied their modern successors. Today the worst penalty for shoddy work is to lose the contract. The inefficient Sumerian contractor sometimes lost his life.

If a builder constructed a house for a seignior, but he did not make his work strong, with the result that the house which he built collapsed and so has caused the death of the owner of the house, the builder shall be put to death.

However, if the collapse of the house caused only destruction of the owner's goods, the builder does not lose his life, but has only to make good the owner's loss. Similarly if a boatbuilder calked a boat so badly that it sprang a leak in the first year, he had to dismantle and strengthen the boat at his own expense. But a bungled surgical operation carried a penalty so severe that one wonders how the surgeon managed to hold his lancet steady.

If a physician performed a major operation on a seignior with a bronze lancet and has caused the seignior's death, or he opened up the eye-socket of a seignior and has destroyed the seignior's eye, they shall cut off his hand.

Other laws are reminiscent of the Mosaic "eye for an eye, a tooth for a tooth".

If a seignior has destroyed the eye of a member of the aristocracy, they shall destroy his eye. . . . If he has broken another seignior's bone, they shall break his bone. . . . If a seignior has knocked out the tooth of a seignior of his own rank, they shall knock out his tooth . . . but if he has knocked out a commoner's tooth he shall pay one-third *mina* of silver.

The laws governing sex relations and marriage are particularly interesting.

If a seignior bound the (betrothed) wife of another seignior, who had had no intercourse with a male and was still living in her father's house, and he has lain in her bosom and they have caught him, that seignior shall be put to death, while that woman shall go free.

If a seignior's wife was accused by her husband but she was not caught while lying with another man, she shall make affirmation by god and return to her house.

The justice of the above statute is balanced by the blatant injustice of the next:

If the finger was pointed at the wife of a seignior but she was not caught while lying with another man, she shall throw herself into the river for the sake of her husband.

Yet other laws in the Code of Hammurabi show an appreciation of women's rights which could hardly be bettered today.

If a seignior wishes to divorce his wife who did not bear him children, he shall give her money to the full amount of her marriage-price and he shall also make good to her the dowry which she brought from her father's house, and then he may divorce her.

and—

If a woman so hated her husband that she has declared "You may not have me" her record shall be investigated by the city council, and if she was careful and not at fault, even though her husband has been going about and disparaging her greatly, that woman, without incurring any blame at all, may take her dowry and go off to her father's house.

but—

If a seignior's wife has brought about the death of her husband because of another man, they shall impale that woman on stakes.

Of course it is impossible to say how many of these laws were strictly enforced; nor can one be sure whether they were the personal edicts of the king or were proposed and passed by a deliberative assembly. Also we know nothing of the judiciary, though "judges" are mentioned in the documents. It would be wrong to think of the Code of Hammurabi as one regards a modern judicial system, in which laws are passed by Parliament and then implemented by an independent judiciary.

Their occasional inconsistency and manner in which they

vary from the humane to the barbarous, suggest to the present writer that they were an accumulation of laws contributed by numerous magistrates over many years; many, while remaining in the "statute book", may well have become obsolete when more civilised counsels prevailed. But this is only a guess.

The translation of the Code of Hammurabi used throughout this chapter is reproduced by courtesy of the Princeton University Press, and is taken from *Ancient Near Eastern Texts* edited by J. B. Pritchard, 1955.

CHAPTER FIFTEEN

THE RELIGION OF SUMER

SUMERIAN art, whether it took the form of literature, architecture, painting, or even in some cases domestic objects, was primarily religious; but not with the meaning we normally attach to that word. Religious beliefs and observances permeated the daily lives of the ancient peoples to a degree which is almost incomprehensible to our modern secular civilisation. Nowadays, in Europe and the United States, religious art has a specific connotation. One thinks of pseudo-Gothic churches, derivative paintings and sculptures of the Holy Family, the Apostles, and the Saints, and the painted and gilded statuettes such as are sold in Lourdes or Rome. There is a self-conscious piety, genuine or bogus, about much modern "religious art". But to the Sumerians or the Ancient Egyptians the worship of God—or "the Gods"—was not something separate from daily life. It was part of it.

A high-born Egyptian lady of 2000 B.C. primped herself in front of a hand-mirror of which the handle was made—most appropriately—in the image of Hat-hor, goddess of love and beauty. An Egyptian scribe, before beginning his day's work, would pour out a libation to Thoth, the god of writing. In the living-rooms of thousands of humble Egyptian homes stood little bronze statuettes of Amun-Re, the sun-god, of Osiris, god of the dead, or of his sister-wife Isis with the infant Horus at her breast. These were not ornaments, nor did they denote any particular piety in the people who owned them. They were necessary companions in the struggle for life; divine creatures who yet shared a certain common humanity with the men and women who worshipped them; they were protectors against evil, intercessors in times of need. The so-called "lucky charms" which superstitious people still carry with them today are their degenerate descendants.

The reasons are very simple. People such as the Sumerians and the Ancient Egyptians were more dependent upon the "forces of nature" than we are. These ancient peoples, however civilised they may have been, were much nearer to primitive man than ourselves. And primitive man, as anthropologists have shown from modern examples, does not regard a "natural force", such as thunder, lightning, rain, flood, pestilence, as an "it". To him it is a "he"—or more often a "she". Professor Frankfort has expressed this point of view very cogently in his book *Before Philosophy*.

There is justification for the aphorism of Crawley; "Primitive man has only one mode of thought, one mode of expression, the *personal*". This does not mean (as is often thought) that primitive man, in order to explain natural phenomena, imparts human characteristics to an inanimate world. Primitive man does not know an inanimate world.

For this reason he does not "personify" the inanimate phenomena. . . . The world appears to primitive man neither inanimate nor empty but abundant with life; and life has individuality, in man or beast or plant, and in every phenomenon which confronts man—the thunderclap, the sudden shower, the eerie unknown clearing in the wood, the stone which suddenly hurls him as he stumbles while on a hunting trip. Any phenomenon may at any time face him, not as It, but Thou.[1]

And if I may be permitted to quote briefly from one of my own books:

[1] Frankfort, W. *Before Philosophy*, Penguin Books, 1954.

If you have to deal with a man much more powerful than yourself, whom you cannot hope to defeat by physical force, you may be able to avoid his anger by propitiating him with gifts. It is much more difficult if you have to cope with the wayward, whimsical, unpredictable ways of a woman. You may, if you are lucky, win her by pleading (prayers) gifts (sacrifice) or flattery (worship). It is significant that the earliest deities seem to have been female.[1]

So it was with the gods and goddesses of ancient Sumer. Consider the forces with which the Sumerians had to come to terms. There was the huge sky which in summer sent down a pitiless blaze which shrivelled life; or in winter poured down violent rainstorms which swelled the rivers, flooded the plain, and drowned men and beasts. There were the great waters upon which their existence depended, but which could also destroy them. And there was the Earth itself, giver of life to men, animals and plants. To the Sumerians these elemental forces were human; Anu was god of the all-encircling sky:

> Oh father of the gods, thy command,
> The very foundation of heaven and earth,
> What God could spurn it?

—they sang in their temples.

The air-god, Enlil, carried out the decrees of the gods and was their war-leader. His cult-centre was at Nippur. The water-god, Enki who wooed the goddess Ninmu, stood for the creative forces of the world, and was also the god of wisdom. The Earth itself was a goddess, as throughout western Asia, Greece and Crete. In Sumer her name was Ki, though sometimes she was called Nintu or "the lady who gives birth". Then there was the moon-god, Nanna, and Inanna, the "Queen of Heaven"—a love-goddess comparable to the Greek Aphrodite. Her brother was the sun-god, Utu. These were some of the principal deities, but there were many

[1] Cottrell, Leonard. *The Anvil of Civilisation*, Faber & Faber, 1958.

others; Ninlil, wife of Enlil, Ninurta, son of Enlil, Lahar, the
cattle-god, Ashnan, the grain-goddess, and so on.

These divinities were not always beneficent, but often cruel
and capricious, like human beings. Sumerian literature,
though it contains many expressions of joy and happiness, is
often pessimistic and fatalistic. Human welfare depends on
the caprices of the gods; a sense of helplessness is apparent in
such passages as:

Mere man—his days are numbered. . . .
Whatever he may do, he is but wind.

—which remind one of Homer's well-known lines:

As is the life of the leaves, so is that of men. The wind
scatters the leaves to the ground; the vigorous forest puts
forth others, and they grow in the spring season. Soon one
generation of men comes and another ceases.

Or, as the Hebrew prophet wrote:

As for man, his days are as grass. . . .

In other passages one is made aware, again and again, of
the terrible destructive power of water, of "the rampant flood
which no man can oppose, which shakes the heavens and
causes earth to tremble. . . . And drowns the harvest in its
time of ripeness."

The contempt of the gods for mankind is expressed in such
myths as that which describes how Enlil broke the earth with
his pick-axe, and as men began to sprout forth like plants,
the other deities gathered round Enlil, imploring him to
allot them serfs from among the new-born men. And in the
Babylonian "Epic of Creation" the god Marduk casually
remarks:

Let him (Man) be burdened with the toil of the gods that
they may freely breathe.

It is not surprising, therefore, that the Sumerians devoted
so much time, wealth and effort to flattering, appeasing, and
interceding with the dread forces which governed their lives.

In every Sumerian city, Lagash, or Eridu, or Nippur, or Kish, the largest and most important buildings were the temples. The principal god or goddess of the city was in fact its ruler, and even the King was only the god's tenant.

The Early Dynastic temple at Khafaja can stand as a typical example of a Sumerian temple.

The life of all [writes Professor Frankfort] was regulated by a calendar which harmonized society's progress through the year with the succession of the seasons. A recurring sequence of religious festivals interrupted all business and routine at frequent intervals; several days in each month were set aside for the celebration of the completion of the moon in one of its phases, and of other natural occurrences. The greatest annual event in each city, which might last as long as twelve days, was the New Year's festival,[1] celebrated at the critical point of the farmer's year when nature's vitality was at a low ebb and everything depended upon a turn of the tide. . . . With great emotional intensity (society) participated by ritual acts in the vicissitudes of the gods in whom were personified the generative forces of nature.[2]

The impressions of Sumerian civilisation which I have attempted to give in this and the preceding chapter are based on our knowledge of Sumer in the "classical" period, i.e. between 2500 and 2000 B.C., but there is little doubt that similar religious practices were current at a much earlier date. For example, when the First Dynasty temple at al 'Ubaid was excavated the archaeologists found an offering table covered with fish-bones six inches deep. Frankfort suggests that this was an offering to Enki, of whom a Sumerian poet writes:

When Enki rose, the fishes rose and adored him.
He stood, a marvel unto the Apsu (Deep),
Brought joy to the Engur (Deep).

[1] The Sumerian New Year is celebrated in the spring.
[2] Frankfort, Henri.

To the sea it seemed that awe was upon him,
To the Great River it seemed that terror hovered around him
While at the same time the south wind stirred the depths of the
Euphrates.[1]

The fact that "the principal god or goddess of the city was, in fact, its ruler" is difficult for modern minds to accept. But it is none the less true. The god owned the land, the High Priest administered the city on his behalf—like the manager of an estate owned by an absentee landlord. We have seen how the god Enlil broke the earth with his pick and so produced men to serve the gods' will. This religious conception is at the heart of Sumerian civic organisation. Since the god ruled, all citizens were equal in his service. Sumerian society was co-operative, with every detail carefully planned. In Sumerian documents the workers on the temple estates, priests, herdsmen, fishermen, gardeners, etc., were referred to as "the people of the god X".

A portion of the temple estates was worked "by all for all". This comprised about one-quarter of the whole and was called *nigenna*-land, which might be translated as "common". Another portion was rented, in allotments, to individuals for their support at a rent which amounted to one-third to one-sixth of the yield. Implements, animals, seed for the Common were supplied by the temple.

High and low worked every year in the "fields of the god", repairing the dykes and canals as a *corvee*. The *sangu*, or priest, who stood at the head of the temple community assigned the shares in the communal tasks. He appeared as bailiff of the god and was assisted by a *nubanda* or steward, who supervised labour, magazines and administration.[2]

I am indebted for this quotation, and some of the material of this chapter, to Professor Frankfort's excellent short book *The Birth of Civilisation in the Near East*, an invaluable and

[1] Translated by T. Jacobsen in *Journal of Near Eastern Studies*, V (1946), p. 140.
[2] Frankfort, H., op. cit.

trustworthy guide to our knowledge of early civilisation. Frankfort also points out that although the rations of barley, wool, etc., issued by the priests were not equal—nor were the tasks assigned to men equally laborious—in principle *all* members of the community were equal. "All received rations as well as allotments to support themselves; all worked on the Common and on the canals and dykes. There was no leisure class. Likewise there were no native serfs."[1] So the *communes* of communist China may not be so modern, after all.

Although some moral teaching entered into Sumerian religion, the greater part of it was concerned with ritual observances of extreme complexity. An Akkadian text dating from the seventh century, but copied from a much older document, gives a detailed account of the temple rituals to be followed "when covering the Temple Kettle-drum". The English translation, given in *Ancient Near Eastern Texts* runs to over 200 lines, of which the following are a few specimens. The text begins:

When you (are confronted with the task of) covering (that is, replacing the head of) the kettledrum (used in the temple) proceed as follows. An expert shall inspect—from head to tip of tail—a sound black bull whose horns and hooves are whole. If its body is black as pitch, it shall be taken for the ceremony. If it is spotted by (as many as?) seven white tufts (which look like) stars, or if it has (ever) been struck with a staff or touched by a goad, it shall not be taken for the ceremony.[2]

The text goes on to describe, in great detail, how the bull must be led into a certain chamber called the "*mummu-house*", the ground swept before it and purified with water, then two bricks have to be laid, one at the right, the other at the left of the doorway leading to the chamber; after this the bull has to be "set on a reed mat, tying his legs with a bond made of goats hair", etc. A further fifty lines describe offering ceremonies involving the use of "seven loaves of barley

[1] Frankfort. H., op. cit.
[2] *Ancient Near Eastern Texts*, op. cit.

bread . . . a paste of honey and cream, dates . . . vessels containing beer and wine, and an offering of roasted meat, with a libation of wine, beer and milk."

Then comes the rite of Washing the Mouth.

You shall draw the curtains shut. On the bull you shall perform the rite of Washing the Mouth. You shall whisper through a reed tube into the bull's left ear the incantation entitled "Alpu ilittu Zi attama". You shall purify the bull, using a brazier and a torch. You shall draw a ring of zisurra-flour around the bull. Standing at its head, you shall sing (the composition called) *Nitugki niginna* to the accompaniment of a bronze *halhalattu*. . . . Then you shall cut open that bull and start a fire with cedar. You shall burn the bull's heart with cedar, cypress and mashatu-flour before the kettledrum. You shall remove the tendon of the left shoulder and shall bury the body of the bull wrapped in a single reed. You shall throw some gunnu-oil on it (and) arrange it so that its face points to the west . . .", etc., etc.

Such ceremonies, similar to those which still survive in parts of modern Asia and Africa (not to mention survivals of European witchcraft) illustrate the yawning gulf which separates us from the civilisations of the ancient world. Charms, spells, incantations may fascinate, amuse or repel us according to our temperaments; but no educated western mind takes them seriously. Yet to these our cultural antecedents, the Sumerians, Babylonians, Egyptians, and even Greeks, they were as essential as what we call "public services"—heat, light, power, hospitals, telephones, petrol stations—are to us, and for the same reason. They kept life going. We can control and harness what we call "natural forces". The Sumerians called these forces "Gods" or "Goddesses" and believed that by ritual observances they could win their support, mitigate their anger and, in effect, harness their power. The modern equivalent of a Sumerian High Priest is not an Archbishop but the head of an atomic energy station.

Sometimes the god appeared to his people in person, as when the statue of the god Anu was carried in procession through the streets of Uruk. This ceremony, too, was governed by exactly-described ritual.

> ... after the statue of the god Anu has left the chapel called Aemenna and has reached the Exalted Gate, all the *masmasu-priests* shall recite three times the incantation (entitled) *Sarru ittasa*. ... After the blessing, the *masmasu-*priests shall (again) recite four times the incantation (entitled) *Sarru ittasu* as far as the Street of the Gods. The *urigallu*-priest, the *masmasu*-priests, the *eribbitu*-priests, and the brewers—who are harnessed to the cross-beam (supporting the moving statue of Anu)—shall bless Anu with the blessing entitled *Anu rabu same u ersetu likrubuka*.

Some northern Protestants may find such rituals strange, but not the peoples of southern Europe. Most visitors to Spain and Italy will recall having seen Roman Catholic ceremonies which bear a close resemblance to these Sumerian and Akkadian street-processions. And all Christians, of whatever denomination, share with the Sumerians a belief in direct intercession with the deity, through prayers and hymns. Some of these prayers have a moving poetry, dignity and beauty; this one, for instance, addressed to the Moon-god, Nanna:

Womb that gives birth to everything, which dwells in a holy habitation with living creatures,

Begetter, merciful in his disposing, who holds in his hand the life of the whole land,

O Lord, whose divinity fills the wide sea with awe, as well as the distant heavens. ...

... Namer of kingships, giver of the sceptre, thou dost determine destiny unto distant days,

O mighty prince, whose deep heart no one of the gods comprehends,

Swift colt whose knees do not tire, who opens the way for his brother gods,

*Whose light goes from the base of heaven to the zenith, who opens
the door of heaven and gives light to all people. . . .*[1]

The Hymn to Nanna is essentially a hymn of praise. Here
is part of a hymn of intercession addressed to "every god".

O Lord, my transgressions are many; great are my sins.
O my god, (my) transgressions are many, great are my sins.
O my goddess (my) transgressions are many; great are my sins.
*O God who I know or do not know (my) transgressions are many;
great are my sins. . . .*

*. . . O my god, merciful one, I address to thee the prayer 'O incline
to me';*
I kiss the feet of my goddess; I crawl before thee. . . .
*How long, O my goddess, whom I know or do not know, ere thy
hostile heart will be quieted.*
Man is dumb; he knows nothing;
Mankind, everyone that exists—what does he know?
Whether he is committing sin or doing good, he does not even know.
O my Lord, do not cast thy servant down. . . .

After the abject servility of this prayer, it is pleasant to turn
to the charming Hymn of Ishtar, goddess of love, composed
by a man who clearly recognised that his goddess was not
only a deity but a woman. Here are the first four verses,
translated by Ferris J. Stephens:

Praise the goddess, the most awesome of the goddesses.
Let one revere the mistress of the people, the greatest of the Igigi[2]
Praise Ishtar, the most awesome of the goddesses,
Let one revere the queen of women, the greatest of the Igigi.

She is clothed with pleasure and love.
She is laden with vitality, charm and voluptuousness.
Ishtar is clothed with pleasure and love.
She is laden with vitality, charm and voluptuousness.

[1] *Ancient Near Eastern Texts*, op. cit., pp. 385–386.
[2] Collective name of the Gods.

In lips she is sweet; life is in her mouth.
At her appearance rejoicing becomes full.
She is glorious; veils are thrown over her head.
Her figure is beautiful; her eyes are brilliant.

The goddess—with her there is counsel.
The fate of everything she holds in her hand.
At her glance there is created joy,
Power, magnificence, the protecting deity and guardian spirit. . . .[1]

*   *   *

Now let us return to the city. It is dawn on New Year's Day. Laboriously we climb the hundreds of steps which mount to the temple, and at each turn we glimpse broader and broader views of the city and the landscape which surrounds it. The men and women in the street wear thick clothing, skirts of sheepskin and woollen cloaks. As we pass under the gate leading to the outer enclosure of the temple and glance back over our shoulder, we see that the wide-spreading fields beyond the city walls look duller and more drab than when we last saw them. The great river is in full spate, and in places the dykes have broken, flooding some outlying fields.

Away to the east the red arc of the sun is just beginning to rise over the rim of the plain, and if we strain our eyes we may see far off the walls and towers of other cities, gilded by the level rays. There is a sound of chanting. The priests are preparing to sacrifice to our patron goddess; and we know that at this same hour, in scores of other towns, smoke is rising from hundreds of Sumerian altars. For this is New Year's Day, when the earth's fertility is renewed, when Anu, master of creation, Enlil, god of the sky, Enki, lord of the waters, and other deities are receiving their due offerings.

The chanting becomes louder as we enter the holiest central enclosure above which the *ziggurat* looms high above us, approached by many flights of steps. It is sacred to Inanna, goddess of love and fertility. The rosy dawn light

[1] *Ancient Near Eastern Texts*, op. cit., p. 383.

gradually pales as a procession of naked priests crosses the enclosure and begins to mount the steps. They are watched by privileged townsfolk in the garments of gold, scarlet and yellow. Each priest carries an offering, a painted urn containing wheat, barley, or wine. Some lead animals for sacrifice. All, from the High Priest to the humblest layman, are reverently fearful.

The High Priest and his acolytes enter the sacred chamber of the Goddess on the topmost platform of the *ziggurat*. Then follows a tense period of waiting, while the sun rises higher in the heavens. Suddenly a murmur breaks out, swelling to a cry of joy. The High Priest is standing on the topmost steps, his hands outstretched. As one man the people crowding the courtyard prostrate themselves. High above them the voice of the *sangu* intones the final prayer, while incense drifts up into the cloudless sky. The ceremony is over. The New Year has begun.

CHAPTER SIXTEEN

SCIENCE AND TECHNIQUES

It is right that this chapter should follow that on Sumerian religion, because the accumulated skill and knowledge which enabled the Sumerians to create a civilisation reposed in the minds of the priestly caste. In Sumeria, as in Ancient Egypt and other early civilisations, the priests were also what we would call the scientists, engineers, physicians, and the guardians of skills and crafts. They were "non-producers" in the material sense, and many believe that they sustained their privileged position by carefully retaining a monopoly of knowledge, which being literate they alone could read, record and transmit. I believe that this is a mistaken view.

The first point to be remembered was that there was no such thing as "abstract" thought or "pure research". Knowledge was usually directed to practical ends. For instance the Babylonians and Chaldaeans, the successors of the Sumerians, were famous for their astronomical and mathematical knowledge. There is a passage in Isaiah (Chapter 47) in which the prophet gloats over the doom of Babylon:

Come down, and sit in the dust, O virgin daughter of Babylon, sit on the ground; there is no throne, O daughter of the Chaldaeans; for thou shalt no more be called tender and delicate. Take the millstones, and grind meal; uncover thy locks, make bare the leg, uncover the thigh, pass over the rivers. Thy nakedness shall be uncovered, yea, thy shame shall be seen. . . .

167

Then Isaiah refers directly to the Chaldaean's known *expertise* in astronomy.

Thou art wearied in the multitude of thy counsels. Let now the astrologers, the stargazers, the monthly prognosticators, stand up, and save thee from these things which shall come upon thee. Behold, thou shalt be as stubble, etc., etc.

This astronomical knowledge, which Babylon had inherited from the Sumerians, was derived from generations of observers who had studied the stars in the clear night skies above Mesopotamia. But their observations had been directed to one end, to measure the season, and by so doing predict the annual rising and flooding of the Twin Rivers. It is true that, at the same time, they had accumulated a body of knowledge regarding the stars on which they based a spurious "science" known as astrology which, unfortunately, still has its modern adherents. But Babylonian and Sumerian astronomy had primarily a severely practical purpose. At the same time there were more imaginative and thoughtful observers who tried to formulate their observations into a general, all-pervading law. This conception of the universe was naturally absorbed into the Sumerian theological system, and it is not easy to separate it from its mythical accretions. Among the scholars who have attempted this feat is Professor S. Kramer, who writes:

The earth, they thought, was a flat disc; heaven, a hollow space enclosed at top and bottom by a solid surface in the shape of a vault. To judge what this heavenly solid was thought to be is still uncertain. To judge from the fact that the Sumerian term for tin is 'metal of heaven' it may have been tin. Between heaven and earth they recognised a substance which they called *lil*, a word whose approximate meaning is "wind" (air, breath, spirit); its most significant characteristics seem to be movement and expansion, and it therefore corresponds to our "atmosphere". The sun, moon, planets, and stars were taken to be made of the same stuff as the atmosphere, but endowed in addition with the quality of luminosity. Surrounding the "heaven-earth" on all sides and at top and bottom was the boundless sea, in which the universe somehow remained fixed and immovable.[1]

The Sumerians attributed the creation of their universe to the gods:

> *After heaven had been moved away from the earth*
> *After earth had been separated from heaven,*
> *After the name of man had been fixed,*
> *After (the heaven-god) An carried off the heaven,*
> *After (the air-God) Enlil carried off the earth. . . .*[2]

Then Enlil and his mother the earth produced men, animals, plants and civilisation. No explanation is given for the heavenly bodies, but since the moon-god Nanna (or Sin) is always regarded as the son of the air-god Enlil, and since Inanna, the moon-goddess, and her brother Utu, the sun-god, are looked upon as the children of Nanna, the Sumerians probably thought of these two heavenly bodies as being created from the moon. One could make an interesting comparison with Artemis and Apollo, in the Graeco-Roman pantheon. The most important point to bear in mind is that these conceptions were not merely "mythological" or "religious" in the modern sense of the words; to the Sumerians they were part of what we would call the "scientific" view of the universe. Although this requires a considerable effort of the imagination it is essential to an understanding of the Sumerian cosmology and cosmogony to recognise that the ideas which we separate into separate compartments labelled "religious" or "scientific" were to the Sumerians indivisible.

Always they thought of the universe as a divine creation, and the kings who ruled Sumer as divinely-inspired.

[1] Kramer, S. N. *History Begins at Sumer*, op. cit., p. 128.

[2] Kramer, S. N. *History Begins at Sumer*, op. cit., p. 134–135.

Oh Sumer, great land, of the lands of the universe,
Filled with steadfast light, dispensing from sunrise to sunset the
divine laws, to (all) people,
Your divine laws are exalted laws, unreachable,
Your heart is profound, unfathomable,
The true learning which you bring . . . like heaven is untouchable,
The king to whom you give birth is adorned with the everlasting
diadem.
The lord to whom you give birth sets ever the crown on his head.
Your lord is an honoured lord; with An, the king, he sits on the
heavenly dais,
Your king is the great mountain, the father Enlil. . . .[1]

Poetry . . . magic . . . religion . . . what have these to do
with science and technique? So the modern rationalist might
inquire. Percy Bysshe Shelley wrote that poets were "the un-
acknowledged legislators of mankind". The remark is often
quoted by people who do not understand its literal truth—so
far as the ancient world was concerned. Professor Kramer has
earnestly endeavoured to separate the wheat of "scientific"
truth from the chaff of poetic myth; in the writer's view, a
vain task. "Your divine laws are exalted laws, unreachable. . . . Your heart is profound, unfathomable. . . . The
true learning which you bring . . . like heaven is untouchable," wrote the unknown Sumerian poet-philosopher whose
words are quoted above. One could attempt to rationalise
his words by saying that they meant, in effect, that only the
priests knew the answers, and that they would take care that
no one else knew them. Knowledge of when to sow and when
to reap, when to prepare for flood-time and when to dig
canals to conserve water, when to build and when to pull
down, when and how to make war and when to negotiate
peace, how to make a *ziggurat*, a palace, a barn or an irriga-
tion-canal . . . all these rested in the minds of a corrupt,
cynical priesthood who traded their technical knowledge in
return for strict acceptance of superstitious beliefs. So the

[1] Kramer, S. N. *History Begins at Sumer*, op. cit., p. 145.

rationalist might argue, but in my view argue wrongly. For I believe that the majority of the priest-technicians themselves believed in what they taught, i.e. that all knowledge comes from God.

Having considered this viewpoint, let us now look at the practical techniques which the Sumerians had mastered, beginning with medicine.

Medicine grew out of magic, and in many cases was indistinguishable from it. At a time when pain and suffering were believed to be caused by hostile deities or malevolent spirits this was understandable—indeed, logical. Therefore many of the magico-medical remedies for disease were accompanied by spells and incantations designed to propitiate or scare away the being who had caused the illness. But the Sumerian physician understood the pharmaceutical value of certain animal, vegetable and mineral substances. Most of these he extracted from plants, e.g. cassia, myrtle, thyme and asafoetida, or from trees such as the pear, fig, date and willow. He used such minerals as potassium nitrate (saltpetre) and sodium chloride (salt).

Kramer mentions a Sumerian tablet found at Nippur which appears to have been part of a medical handbook or pharmacopoeia. With the help of a young Philadelphia chemist, Dr. Martin Levy, Kramer made a close study of the tablet, and was able to establish that

> the remedies prescribed . . . were both salves and filtrates to be applied externally, and liquids to be taken internally. The usual instructions for compounding salves were to pulverize one or more simples, to infuse the powder with "ku-shumma" wine, and to spread both common tree oil and cedar oil over the mixture. . . . As for those remedies which were to be taken internally, beer was usually the vehicle chosen to make them palatable to the patient. The several simples were ground to powder and dissolved in beer for the sick man to drink.[1]

[1] Kramer, S. N. *History Begins at Sumer*, op. cit., pp. 101–102.

From certain instructions given in the tablet it would seem that the Sumerian doctors were familiar with quite elaborate chemical processes, e.g. how to separate the chemical components of natural substances. But the document cannot compare with the famous Egyptian Medical Papyrus, which gives not only the names of drugs to be used, but the diseases against which they were believed to be effective. The Egyptian document also describes how to make a diagnosis, how to recognise symptoms, and make a prognosis. This is not to suggest that Sumerian medicine was necessarily less advanced than that of Ancient Egypt; only that, up to date, there is insufficient evidence on which to base a firm opinion.

But from the literature of the later Babylonians, who derived much of their knowledge from Sumer, we know that they possessed a considerable knowledge of anatomy—derived no doubt from the ritual dissection of animals during sacrifices—and were competent surgeons. Sumerian skulls sometimes show evidence of skilful "trepanning", i.e. removing a portion of the skull to relieve pressure on the brain, and then replacing the segment which had been cut out. But such skills were known among primitive peoples with no claim to a high civilisation. Surgical instruments have been discovered, including knives and lancets which appear to have been developed from weapons of war, and forceps which may have been modified from women's toilet instruments.

In the field of engineering—especially hydraulic engineering—we are on firmer ground, for it is doubtful if any people in the world, save the Egyptians, were as skilful as the Sumerians in the management and control of water. Their very existence depended on this skill, for unless the floodwaters of the Tigris and Euphrates were controlled, directed and conserved by canals and ditches, the country could not have supported its enormous population. The proudest boasts of the Sumerian kings and governors was that they built, repaired or extended canals. Even today, flying over southern Iraq, one can still see the criss-cross pattern of these innumerable channels, now mostly dried up, though some

still survive and are in use. Even as late as the fifth century
B.C. Herodotus admiringly wrote of the land:

It is so bountiful in its yield of those fruits which men call
cereal that it returns for the most part two-hundred-fold,
and, at the best, even three-hundred-fold. The breadth of
the blades of wheat and barley there easily reaches four
fingers. And of millet and sesame what the size is—as it
were that of a tree—though I know well, I will not mention, being sure that, for those who have never visited
Babylonia, even so much as I have said already as to its
fruits will have gone far beyond the measure of belief.

Sumerian literature abounds in references to land cultivation and the skill needed to produce a maximum yield. In
the "Wisdom Literature", comparable to the Hebrew proverbs, one finds sayings like these:

Fruit in the spring (of the year)—fruit of mourning [in
other words] soon ripe, soon rotten.[1]
A canal in the direction of the wind brings water in
abundance.[1]

Keep an eye on the man who puts in the barley seed that he
makes the seed fall two fingers uniformly.

When you are about to cultivate your field, take care to
open the irrigation works (so that) their water does not rise
too high in it (the field). When you have emptied it of
water, watch the field's wet ground that it stays even; let no
wandering ox trample it. . . . When the field is burning (in
the summer sun) let it be divided up into equal parts. Let
your tools hum with activity. . . .[2]

What would—and did eventually—happen to Sumeria if
this work was neglected or destroyed is movingly foretold by
a Sumerian poet:

In canal-boat towpaths grow nothing but weeds,

[1] *Ancient Near Eastern Texts,* op. cit., p. 425.
[2] Kramer, S. N. *History Begins at Sumer,* op. cit., p. 109.

Its chariot-roads grew nothing but the "wailing-plant"
Moreover, on its canal-boat towpaths and landings
No human being walks because of the wild-goats, vermin, snake,
    and mountain-scorpion.
The plains where grew the heart-soothing plants, grew nothing but
    "reeds of tears",
Agade, instead of its sweet-flowing water, there flowed bitter
    water,
Who said "I would dwell in that city" found not a good dwelling-
    place.
Who said "I would lie down in Agade" found not a good sleeping-
    place. . . .

The Sumerians' skill as builders has already been described in preceding chapters, but something may be said
concerning the methods of their architects. Their buildings
were obviously based on accurate plans and drawings. A
statue of Gudea, Governor of Lagash, now in the Paris
Louvre, shows such a plan resting on the Governor's lap.
Such skill argues an accurate system of measuring dimensions, weights and capacities.

The statue of Gudea shows sixteen fingers or digits of the
Sumerian cubit, a standard of measurement reckoned by the
French metrologist, Thureau Dangin, as 495 mm. or
19·488 in. This was the cubit of the *ziggurat* of Babylon and
that of Ur. (The Egyptian "royal cubit" was 523 mm. or
20·63 in.) The modern descendant of the Sumerian cubit is
the Persian *arish* (varying from 38·97 in.—990 mm. to 38·6 in.
—981 mm.) The Syrian-Babylonian log (33 cubic inches or
541 cubic centimetres) was 0·95 of an imperial pint. Four
logs were equivalent to one *kab* or *kapitha*, or 132 cubic
inches or 2·165 litres. Although these are Babylonian mea-
sures they may also have been used by Sumerian traders and
merchants.

Sumerian proficiency in mathematics, which the Babylonians inherited and developed, probably originated in the
necessity for the accurate measurement of land boundaries

when these were liable to be washed away by floods. The requirements of trade and taxation provided an additional stimulus. In the time of Hammurabi, when Babylon was a thriving commercial centre, the Babylonians used both a decimal and a sexagesimal system. Even today our clocks and watches divide time into units of sixty seconds to the minute and sixty minutes to the hour; we owe this to the Babylonians' sexagesimal system of numeration. They were acquainted with arithmetical and geometrical series, and had an elementary knowledge of proportion. Their experience of astronomy led them to divide a circle into 360 parts, and they knew that the circumference of a circle is (approx.) six times its radius. They tabulated multiplication, division, square and cube roots, and some of their tablets contain mathematical problems for solution by students. Yet it would be wrong to suggest that they were interested, as were the Greeks, in "pure" mathematics.

Their mathematical techniques had been developed to meet severely practical needs. They studied the stars in order to measure time, which was necessary for the observation of seasonal religious festivals and the planting and reaping of crops; also because they believed that the stars affected the lives of mankind. They developed systems of measurement (*a*) for the division of land (*b*) for the planning of buildings (*c*) for determining the weight, bulk and quantity of commodities for sale, purchase and exchange.

But, bubbling to the surface of all this agricultural, commercial, and mercantile activity rose a delicate, perfumed froth—those delectable "non-essential" articles produced by artists and craftsmen, such as the frivolous, absurd, and beautiful head-dress of Queen Shub-ad. Such things, which doctrinaire Marxists condemn as symbols of "conspicuous consumption" are none the less true products of civilisation. There is no need to describe them; the illustrations of the goldwork, jewellery, inlay, etc., found by Woolley at Ur convey more than any words can describe. The best that these unknown Sumerian artists created is equal to the finest

products of Ancient Egypt, not only in delicacy and craftsmanship, but in sheer elegance and sophistication of design.

Some scholars tend to sneer at the layman's absorption in
these more "glamorous" archaeological discoveries, alleging
that he ignores the dungy soil from which such delicate
flowers grew. But may not the layman's instinct be right? It
is possible that, five thousand years from today, human beings
may still admire the lines of a fine aeroplane or motor-car
produced in the twentieth century. But will any spare a
thought for the thousands, in offices, foundries, laboratories
and machine-shops, whose efforts produced the finished
article? I doubt it.

CHAPTER SEVENTEEN

ART, MUSIC, LITERATURE

EXAMPLES of the architecture and art of Sumer have been described and illustrated in previous chapters, together with random quotations from its very considerable poetic literature. The present chapter can only be a brief summary. Readers who wish to pursue these subjects further are invited to study the Bibliography especially *The Development of Sumerian Art* by Sir Leonard Woolley and (for Sumerian literature) such works as *Ancient Near Eastern Texts*, published by the Princeton University Press, 1955, and Professor Kramer's *Sumerian Mythology* and *History Begins at Sumer*.

From the earliest known period at which monumental architecture is found, down to the time of the Babylonians, (who succeeded to the civilisation of Sumer) the main elements in both religious and secular buildings were a number of chambers opening on to a central court, or series of courts. Temples, like all other buildings, were of mud-brick of the "plano-convex" type, mainly sun-dried, but where a harder material was needed for pavements or revetments, kiln-baked bricks were used. Decoration was colourful and elaborate; it might consist of a patterned mosaic of vari-coloured cones and pictorial inlays, and sometimes—as in the case of the First Dynasty temple at al 'Ubaid, there was a frieze of heraldic figures, of copper or gold, overlaying a core of bitumen. These buildings had arched doorways and flat roofs approached by staircases. From the earliest times the façades were divided into buttresses and recessed, probably a survival of the primitive reed-built dwellings of the earliest settlers.

This "recess and buttress" or "panelled-façade" style, so characteristic of Sumerian architecture, is also found in the Early Dynastic Period of Ancient Egypt, *c.* 3000 B.C., and a connection between the two seems certain.

The temple rooms were furnished with offering-tables, niches for the cult-statues, braziers, and—a peculiar feature of Sumerian temples—benches on which stood statues of important officials. The idea underlying this practice was that the people thus represented were, vicariously, always in the sacred presence. These statues represent some of the finest examples of Sumerian portraiture. The early ones are highly conventionalised, but as a civilisation progressed they became more and more naturalistic, with painted hair and inlaid eyes. Still later, however, the Sumerian artists returned to a rigid formalism.

The main buildings of the temple stood within a large walled enclosure; sometimes two enclosures one inside the other. Subsidiary buildings housed the innumerable priests and officials who administered the temple estates. If a modern western man found himself in a Sumerian city of 2500 B.C., he would be astonished by the number of priests and priestly officials thronging its streets. (Perhaps the nearest comparison would be with modern Burma or Thailand, where every other man seems to be a saffron-robed monk.) From both Sumerian and Babylonian records we know a great deal about this immense religious hierarchy. One class—the kalu-priests—were responsible for the temple chants; another, the baru-priests, took the omens which played a highly important part in Sumerian religious life. No enterprise, however small, was undertaken without reading the omens. These were of various kinds, ranging from the examination of the liver of a sacrificed animal to observing the flight of birds or even noting the pattern made by pouring oil from a jar. There were other priests responsible for ritual ablutions, and among the numerous priestesses some were princesses and ladies of high rank. In about 3000 B.C., 736 persons served the goddess Ba'u, but in later Babylonian times the god Marduk had a staff numbering more than 3,000.

Statues of men and women in an attitude of adoration occur frequently in religious Sumerian art. Sometimes they are shown standing, eyes fixed straight ahead, as if gazing at the object of worship. Others, such as the early statues from Tell Asmar, are kneeling, feet awkwardly tucked beneath their buttocks. In other cases the posture of the hands is the same, clasped together in front of the breast. So the worshippers must have looked as they stood or knelt in the temples sacred to their city's gods.

Stone ritual vessels were also sometimes carved in relief. The quality of this sculpture varies greatly. There is a limestone vase from a store of temple vessels found in a lower *Jemdet Nasr* level at Warka, and as it had been repaired it may well have belonged to the earlier *Uruk* period. It shows figures of lions grouped round a tree; while the figures are vigorously carved, the whole composition is clumsy and out of balance. On the other hand other large decorated vases, found by German archaeologists at the same site, reveal no such faults, the stiff, conventionalised figures being perfectly adapted to the shape of the vessel and the texture of the stone.

> The composition is formal [writes Woolley] and the conventions are such as we must expect in Sumerian art—a disregard of perspective, a sacrifice of scale to the need of covering the whole field of ornament, a somewhat hieratic stiffness which in less skilful hands would result in monotony; but with this an extremely fine sense of proportion and a thorough understanding of the real nature of relief.[1]

Even finer, in the present writer's view, is the fragment of a large decorated gypsum vase, also found at Warka, which

[1] Woolley, Sir Leonard. *The Development of Sumerian Art*, Faber & Faber, 1935.

shows a procession of men bearing offerings, and in the lower frieze animals going to the sacrifice. The artist who sculptured these figures knew how to adapt his technique to his material and produce, with the utmost economy of line, the same hard, muscular strength which one finds in the best Egyptian sculpture of the Old Kingdom.

Turning from temples to private dwellings, we find again the simple principle of erecting buildings round a central court; though these became larger and more elaborate as Sumerian cities grew in size and importance. Sometimes there was a roofed central hall with clerestory lighting. In some secular public buildings colonnades gave shade, and provided the architect with an opportunity for charming coloured mosaic decoration, which gave a scintillating, jewel-like effect. A splendid example of this is the columned wall of the *Uruk* period found at Warka.

The general visual effect of a Sumerian city of the historical period (between 2800–2000 B.C.) would be of hard, rectilinear shapes—straight streets, block-like buildings with flat roofs, surrounded by a thick buttressed wall. And this angularity would be emphasised by the fierce sunlight and black shadows. That is the effect one gets today when a buried city has been cleared of debris; but now we are looking only at the bare skeleton, stripped of the colour and glitter which once relieved its austerity.

Inside the dwellings we would be surprised, perhaps, by the relative lack of furniture, even in the richest homes. But what we did see would be of elegant design and finely made; some of the furniture was inlaid with tortoiseshell, and inset with decorative patterns made from red carnelian and blue lapis. There would be gaily painted pottery, often with designs of animals and birds, and in the more sumptuous homes, delicately fluted drinking vessels of gold and silver such as were found in the royal graves at Ur.

Standing on a low table we might see a lovely shallow bowl of translucent green calcite, a blue cup fashioned from a single piece of lapis-lazuli, and in a corner, on its metal

stand, one of those tall, graceful jars of veined alabaster used
for storing wine. Nearby stands one of the splendid lyres or
harps, its gold mountings catching the sunlight, the delicate
shell inlay echoing that of the elaborate gaming-board
which rests on a table between two bearded players. Of the
clothing, head-dresses and jewellery worn by these Sumerian
men and women we have already caught glimpses.

The presence of the harp reminds us that the Sumerians
were a musical people. The oldest example of musical nota-
tion in the world is a Sumerian hymn recorded on a tablet
of c. 800 B.C. Unfortunately it still continues to defy satisfactory interpretation. Much of Sumerian music was, of course,
religious; hymns, chants, and sacred dances, but secular
music undoubtedly existed.

> Religion [writes Mr. Crossley-Holland] has played a
> dominant part in shaping musical systems and creating
> musical forms which, spreading out into secular life, have
> helped to mould the music of the courts and the people
> also. . . . Like the other arts, it is regarded as a ritual
> means of preparing the human personality for perceiving
> metaphysical truths, and thus has, in its turn, been much
> moulded by efforts to perceive these very truths.

Although the original music of Sumer, as of Egypt and the
Middle East generally, cannot be interpreted through the
documents, or even by the instruments which have survived,
it is extremely likely that elements of it live on in the music
played by the present-day occupants of Mesopotamia. This
seems to me highly probable. If building-methods, tools,
agricultural implements and methods, have survived the passage of some 5,000 years, there seems reason to suppose that
music also may have survived, though in a somewhat altered
form. A well-known German musicologist has traced, with
some conviction, elements of Ancient Egyptian music which
still persist in the songs of the peasants of the Upper Nile.
If this is true of Egypt, why not of Sumer? The instruments
found in Sumerian tombs, the harp, the lyre, pipes, drums,

etc., have close equivalents in Western Asia and Africa to-day. My belief is that Sumerian music, like modern Arab music, was strongly percussive, atonal, making great use of the flexibility of the human voice, with subtle and complex rhythms produced by drums and stringed instruments.

But the human voice would predominate. The types of instruments depicted in Sumerian reliefs and found by Woolley at Ur, were more suitable for accompaniment than for solo performance, though no doubt there were instrumental obligatos as in modern Oriental music. When one reads the lovely Sumerian songs and poems, such as the love-song reproduced at the end of this chapter, one should imagine them sung to an accompaniment of plucked strings—and, in the case of dances, of drums.

But who is the owner of this Sumerian house? Who can afford to commission such works of high craftsmanship, and possess the cultured taste needed for their appreciation? We can attempt an answer. In 1946 Nikolaus Schneider, a well-known German linguist, compiled from Sumerian documents of about 2000 B.C., a list of some five hundred scribes, with the names of their fathers. From this we know the kind of people who could afford to give their sons what would now be called a University education. Among the occupations listed are these:

> Governors
> "City Fathers"
> Ambassadors
> Sea Captains
> Military officers
> High Tax Officials
> Priests
> Accountants
> Managers
> Supervisors.

The imaginary Sumerian home into which we have looked might belong to any one of these men, though from the extreme richness of its furnishings it is likely to belong to a Governor or high civic official.

From another part of the house, across the sunlit courtyard, come the voices of young children, playing with the same kind of toys which amuse present-day boys and girls; model wagons and chariots, dolls and toy animals, examples of which have been found in Sumerian graves. As these are the children of higher-ranking families, the boys will undoubtedly be attending one of the Temple schools to learn the art of writing which is the foundation of higher education.

We know that schools or colleges existed from the numerous examples of school textbooks, exercises, etc., which have been found among the cuneiform tablets. We can also trace the development of these colleges from being mere appendages of the temple, concerned only with the professional training of scribes and officials, to something more nearly approaching the modern conception of a University. In the later part of this chapter I acknowledge a profound debt to the American scholar, Professor S. N. Kramer, most persuasive of Sumerologists. Not only is he responsible for translating and publishing numerous hitherto-unknown Sumerian texts, but in his books *Sumerian Mythology* and particularly *History Begins at Sumer* he exhibits a most engaging faculty for communicating his own enthusiasm for Sumerian literature to the lay reader.

As we have seen, the first elementary pictograms were probably invented by the *Uruk* people and developed by their successors, the *Jemdet Nasr* folk. But at the time we are now considering, between 2500 and 2000 B.C. the Sumerian language had developed into a subtle and sensitive instrument of communication, with a complex grammar and extensive vocabulary. As in Ancient Egypt (where similar schools existed) no one could hope to rise to high rank in the administration until he had command of the language. Boys were put to school at an early age and stayed there until they were young men.

... in the course of its development [writes Kramer] the school came to be the centre of culture and learning in Sumer. Within its walls flourished the scholar-scientist, the man who studied whatever theological, botanical, zoological, mineralogical, geographical, grammatical and linguistic knowledge current in his day, and who in some cases added to this knowledge.... Moreover, rather unlike present-day institutions of learning, the Sumerian school was also the centre of what might be called creative writing. It was here that the literary creations of the past were studied and copied; here, too, that new ones were composed. While it is true that the majority of graduates from the Sumerian schools were scribes in the service of the temples and palace, and among the rich and powerful of the land, there were some who devoted their lives to teaching and learning.[1]

There exists, on a clay tablet, an essay about a Sumerian schoolboy written round about 2000 B.C. Probably composed by a schoolmaster, it begins with the master questioning the pupil as follows:

"Schoolboy, where did you go from the earliest days?"
"I went to school"
"What did you do in school?"[2]

The pupil's reply includes the following:

"I recited my tablet, ate my lunch, prepared my (new) tablet, wrote it, finished it; and then they assigned me my oral work, and in the afternoon they assigned me my written work. When school was dismissed, I went home, and found my father sitting there. I told my father of my written work, then recited my tablet to him, and my father was delighted. When I woke early in the morning, I faced my mother and said to her 'Give me my lunch, I want to go to school'. My mother gave me two 'rolls' and I

[1] Kramer, S. N. *History Begins at Sumer*, Thames & Hudson, 1958.
[2] Kramer, S. N., op. cit.

set out. . . . In school the monitor in charge said to me 'Why are you late?' Afraid and with pounding heart, I entered before my teacher and made a respectful curtsey."[1]

The rest of this document makes it clear that the pupil was in bad odour with his teacher, who tells him that his "hand (copy) is not satisfactory" and then gives him the cane. The boy then consults his father and suggests that the teacher be invited home. This the parent does, and then follows a most amusing scene, in which the teacher, having been given an excellent dinner, and presented with "a new garment, a gift . . . and a ring" decides to take a more sympathetic view of his pupil. The tablet ends with the reassuring words, addressed by master to student:

"Young man, because you did not neglect my word, did not forsake it, may you reach the pinnacle of the scribal art, may you achieve it completely. . . . Of your brothers may you be their leader, of your friends may you be their chief, may you rank the highest of the schoolboys. . . . You have carried out well the school's activities, you have become a man of learning."

What were these "tablets" which the schoolboy had to study and copy? There were two main groups. The first was scientific and scholarly—grammatical texts, lists of Sumerian words and phrases, lists of names of plants, animals, insects, birds, cities, countries, stones, minerals. There were also mathematical tables and problems. The second group consisted of ancient Sumerian epic poems, the literary importance of which is becoming increasingly recognised. Apart from the myths and legends of Ancient Egypt, these Sumerian poems comprise the earliest known literature in the world, and some of them have an almost Homeric splendour and vitality. Moreover, unlike say the Old Testament, the *Rigveda* of India, the *Avesta* of ancient Persia, and Homer's

[1] Kramer, S. N., op. cit.

Odyssey and *Iliad*, the Sumerian tablets have come down to us unaltered and unedited since the scribes inscribed them some 4,000 years ago.

These "literary texts" comprise less than *one per cent* of the 250,000 tablets unearthed in Mesopotamia during the past century. The remaining 99% are mainly economic in character, e.g. contracts of sale, notes and receipts, lists of workers and their wages, business letters, wills and testaments. Of the 1% of purely literary tablets (about 3,000 in all) about 2,000 were excavated by the American archaeologists at Nippur, and of these 1,100 now rest in the University Museum of Pennsylvania. Of the rest, about 500 are split between the British and Berlin Museums, and others are in the Paris Louvre. A few are in private collections and in Istanbul. Many of these valuable Sumerian documents are still uncopied and untranslated.

There is also a relatively small group of dedicatory inscriptions on steles, bricks, cones, vases, etc., which provide us with most of the political history outlined in the final chapter of this book. But undoubtedly the most significant documents of Sumer, so far as its religion and culture are concerned, are those unearthed by the Americans at Nippur fifty or more years ago.

The language in which these documents are written still presents a puzzle to linguists. It is not Semitic. It is not Indo-European—i.e. it does not belong to the group of tongues from which nearly all European and Indian languages are descended. "It belongs" writes Kramer, "to the so-called agglutinative type of languages exemplified by Turkish, Hungarian and Finnish, but none of these languages . . . seems to have a close affiliation with Sumerian."

Probably the language would never have been translated but for the fact that the Accadians, a Semitic people who eventually became dominant in Sumer, preserved it for literary and religious purposes, as Latin and Ancient Greek have been preserved in the modern world. The new people compiled bilingual syllabries and dictionaries with Sumerian words translated into Accadian. As this was a Semitic language related to numerous living tongues, it was not too difficult to translate, so these bilingual texts provided the basic material for a translation of Sumerian. None the less, since Accadian and Sumerian are so completely different in grammar and vocabulary, accurate translation was never easy, and still presents many problems.

Another formidable difficulty arose from the fragmented state of many of the texts. We have seen how George Smith (Chapter Five) had to make a journey to Mesopotamia to search for the missing fragment of the "Flood" tablet. He was lucky to find it. Quite often scholars have had to reconstruct the text of a poem from many fragmented tablets, adding a bit of one to a bit of another. Fortunately the Sumerian scribes made many copies of the same text. The Sumerian schoolboys and apprentice scribes, laboriously copying and re-copying the same hymn or poem, (often inaccurately) have been of great assistance to the modern linguist. For instance the famous "Lamentation on the Destruction of Ur" was reconstructed from twenty-two fragments. Kramer used forty-nine pieces to reconstruct the poem called "The Feats and Exploits of Ninurta".

What does this literature consist of? It can be divided roughly into (a) epics and myths, (b) hymns, (c) poems in praise of gods or kings and (d) "Words of Wisdom"—like the Hebrew proverbs. I have already quoted extracts from the "Epic of Gilgamesh", the "Story of the Deluge", the "Descent of Inanna into the Underworld" and the wooing of the goddess Ninmu by the god Enki. There is only space for a few more specimen quotations, but readers anxious to pursue the subject further will find ample material in the books recommended earlier in this chapter and in the Bibliography. There is much to discover and a study of parallels between Sumerian and later literature, e.g. Hebrew and Greek, would provide much food for reflection. For instance, there is a passage from "Gilgamesh, Enkidu and the Nether World" which seems to foreshadow Genesis:

After heaven had been moved away from earth,
After earth had been separated from heaven
After the name of man had been fixed,
After (the heaven-god) Anu carried off the heaven,
After (the air-god) Enlil carried off the earth . . . etc.

The parallels between the stories of Noah and Utnapishtim need no emphasis, nor those between the description of the Sumerian Paradise and that of the Bible:

"In Dilmun (Paradise) the raven utters no cry,
The ittidu-*bird utters not the cry of the* ittidu-*bird*
The lion kills not
The wolf snatches not the lamb,
Unknown is the kid-devouring wild dog,
Unknown is the grain-devouring . . .
Unknown is the widow . . .
. . . The sick-eyed says not "I am sick-eyed"
The sick-headed says not "I am sick-headed"
Its (Dilmun's) old woman says not "I am an old
woman"
Its old man says not "I am an old man" . . .[1]

There is another extraordinary poem which Kramer copied in 1951–1952 when he was at Istanbul as Fulbright Research Professor; its reproach to God for undeserved suffering strongly recalls the Book of Job. Here is a specimen passage:

I, the wise, why am I bound to the ignorant youths?
I, the discerning, why I am counted among the ignorant?
Food is all about, yet my food is hunger,
On the day shares were allotted to all, my allotted
share was suffering. . . .

And again:

My god, the day shines bright over the land, for me
the day is black,

[1] Kramer, S. N. *History Begins at Sumer*, op. cit.

The bright day, the good day . . . . has . . . like the . . . .
Tears, lament, anguish and depression are lodged
within me,
Suffering overwhelms me like one chosen for nothing
but tears,
Evil fate holds me in its hand, carries off my breath
of life,
Malignant sickness bathes my body . . . .

Among the "Wisdom" literature is this:

Who possess much silver may be happy
Who possesses much barley, may be happy,
But who has nothing at all, can sleep.

and:

A restless woman in the house
Adds ache to pain.

It is probably the same sufferer who wrote:

For his pleasure; marriage.
On his thinking it over; divorce.

There is a manual on farming which includes such instructions as—"Keep an eye on the man who puts in the barley seed that he makes the seed fall two fingers uniformly" and "Where you have ploughed straight furrows, plough now diagonal furrows". There is an interesting reference in this document to the complex irrigation system on which Sumerian farming depended:

When you are about to cultivate your field, take care to open the irrigation works (so that) their water does not rise too high in it (the field). When you have emptied it of water, watch the field's wet ground so it stays even; let no wandering ox trample it. Chase the prowlers and have it treated as settled land. . . .

Cylinder seals often show scenes of ploughing and other agricultural activities.

Tales of heroism, moral reflections, legal documents, reports of court cases, accounts of war and diplomacy, besides hymns, prayers and lamentations, are among the treasures awaiting those who wish to enter the rich and expanding field of Sumerian literature. For the beginner there is no better guide than Professor Kramer, who is responsible for the translations I have quoted in this chapter.

Love-poems are rare in translated Sumerian writings, though who knows how many may still be lying in dusty Museum cupboards awaiting translation? The one I have chosen to end this chapter is startling in its beauty, reaching out to us across the dead centuries like the warm arms of a lover.

> *Bridegroom, dear to my heart,*
> *Goodly is your beauty, honeysweet.*
> *Lion, dear to my heart,*
> *Goodly is your beauty, honeysweet . . .*
>
> *. . . Bridegroom, let me caress you,*
> *My precious caress is more savoury than honey.*
> *In the bedchamber, honey-filled,*
> *Let me enjoy your goodly beauty.*
> *Lion, let me caress you,*
> *My precious caress is more savoury than honey.*
>
> *Bridegroom, you have taken your pleasure of me.*
> *Tell my mother, she will give you delicacies,*
> *Tell my father, he will give you gifts.*
>
> *Your spirit, I know where to cheer your spirit,*
> *Bridegroom, sleep in our house until dawn.*
> *Your heart, I know where to gladden your heart,*
> *Lion, sleep in our house until dawn.*[1]

[1] Copied by Muazzez Cig, of the Istanbul Museum; translated by S. N. Kramer in *History Begins at Sumer*.

CHAPTER EIGHTEEN

POLITICAL HISTORY

As we have noted, the political history of early dynastic Sumer, its wars, conquests, alliances and dynastic changes, is contained in about 600 inscriptions, mostly carved on stone in the form of commemorative steles or building dedications. Historiography in the modern sense was unknown, and most of the records which have survived are bald accounts of the names of kings and notables; who built this temple, conquered this city, or subjugated this territory. There are, however, among the "literary" tablets, some which give accounts of wars and diplomatic negotiation between city and city, when Sumer was divided. Later there are accounts of the great Accadian conqueror Sargon, who unified the entire land and expanded its influence by force of arms, from the Mediterranean to the mountains of Turkey, Persia and Lebanon.

From these it is possible to trace an outline of Sumerian political history. For several centuries city struggled with city; frequently these wars arose out of disputes concerning land divisions, trade and territory.

For instance Professor Kramer quotes an interesting document which he translated in the Museum of the Ancient Orient, in Istanbul. Written about 4,000 years ago, it is a Sumerian heroic poem which deals with a dispute between two kings, Enmerkar of Erech and the Lord of Aratta. These two rulers lived possibly more than a thousand years

before the tablet was written, and though, like most documents of this age, it is clouded by obscure religious sym-
bolism, one can see that it deals basically with a power-
struggle.

Enmerkar was king of Erech, between the Tigris and
Euphrates. Aratta, another city-state, lay far to the east, in
the mountains of what is now Persia. Seven mountain ranges
lay between the two states, yet Aratta perched on a lonely
hill-top, was threatened with war by the ruler of Erech. The
reasons for this are not immediately clear. The poem, written
in a roundabout style, begins by praising the greatness of
Erech which, the poet states, was favoured by the goddess
Inanna. Enmerkar implores the goddess to make the people
of Aratta bring gold, silver, lapis-lazuli and carnelian, and
to build for him temples and shrines. Inanna advises him to
send a messenger or herald across the seven ranges of mountains, bearing a message for the lord of Aratta ordering him
to carry out the goddess's instructions under the threat of
war.

Inanna, the queen of all the lands,
Says to Enmerkar, the son of Utu;
"Come, Enmerkar, instruction I would offer you, take my instruc-
    tion,
A word I would speak to you, give ear to it!
Choose a word-wise herald from . . .
Let him ascend the . . . mountains,
Let him descend the . . . mountains,
Before the . . . of Anshan,
Let him prostrate himself like a young singer,
Awed by the dread of the great mountains,
Let him wander about in the dust—
Aratta will submit to Erech;
The people of Aratta,
Having brought down the stones of the mountains from their land,
Will build for you the great chapel, set up for you the great shrine,
Cause to appear for you the great shrine, the shrine of the gods,

Who adorns the daises of the highland Shuba
Because the lord, my king, who is her servant,
Made her the "Queen of Eanna".
"The lord of Aratta will submit"—
Thus said to him in the brickwork of Kullah.
Then was the lord depressed, deeply pained,
He had no answer, he kept seeking an answer,
At his own feet he cast a troubled eye, he finds an answer. . . .[1]

The answer which the lord of Aratta sent was a suggestion that, instead of war, there should be a contest between two selected champions. But he added that, since Inanna had turned against him, he was prepared to carry out Enmerkar's request if the latter would send him large quantities of grain. Hear again one detects the true economic basis of the dispute. Enmerkar, living in his mud-brick city, has no building stone, but his wide fields yield an abundance of grain, of which mountainous Aratta is short. Enmerkar agrees and sends the grain, which, says the poet, was "poured into the courtyard of the palace". At this the people of Aratta were delighted, and ready to carry out Enmerkar's request. But their king, who seems to have been an unstable weakling, sent back an hysterical answer in which he demanded from Enmerkar the same tribute of carnelian and lapis-lazuli which the king of Erech had asked of him. The negotiations continued for a considerable time, and one feels sorry for the unfortunate herald who had to keep crossing those seven ranges of mountains to carry threats and counter-threats between the two petty monarchs. Again Enmerkar threatened war unless the lord of Aratta delivered "the stones of the mountains" to build and decorate the shrine at Eridu. In the end—according to the poem—the people of Aratta complied with Enmerkar's "request" and brought "gold, silver and lapis-lazuli" to Erech.

Yet it would seem that, even at this early period, round

[1] Kramer, S. N. *History Begins at Sumer*, Thames & Hudson, 1958. Pp. 60–65.

Carry out for you your divine laws in Kullah,
Fashion for you the Abzu like a holy highland,
Purify for you Eridu like a mountain,
Cause to appear for you the holy chapel of the ⸗
    vern. . . ."

Enmerkar told the herald to warn the lord
what would befall his city if these tasks were not

Oh, herald, speak unto the lord of Aratta and say ur
"I will make the people of that city flee like the . . .
    tree,
I will make it (Aratta) desolate like a place of . . .
I will make it hold dust like an utterly destroyed city,
Aratta that habitation which Enki has cursed—
I will surely destroy the place, like a place which has
    stroyed. . . ."

Stripped of its religious and poetical clothing, thi
tells the old familiar story of the "haves" and the
nots". Enmerkar wanted to build enduring monume
stone. Erech had neither stone nor craftsmen capable of
it. Aratta had both, besides rich minerals. So Enm
tries to get them by threatening violence, coupled wi
stroke of psychological warfare; the goddess Inanna, he s
prefers Erech to Aratta. At first the lord of Aratta does
believe this, and says to the herald:

Oh herald, speak unto your king, the lord of Kullah, and say ur
    him
"Me, the lord fit for the pure hand,
She, who is the royal . . . of heaven, the queen of heaven and earth,
The mistress of all the divine laws, the holy Inanna,
Has brought me to Aratta, the land of the holy divine laws,
Has made me close the 'face of the highland' like a large door;
How then shall Aratta submit to Erech?"

But the herald answers him:

The great queen of heaven, who rides the fearful divine laws,
Who dwells in the mountains of the highland Shuba,

about 3000 B.C., the monarchs were not always absolute, but sometimes referred to "the convened elders of the city". Moreover, there appear to have been two "houses", an Upper House or Senate composed of the city elders, and a Lower House consisting of men able to bear arms. Kramer quotes a fragment of another tablet describing how the hero Gilgamesh, lord of Erech, consulted the two assemblies when his city was threatened by its great rival, the town of Kish.

> *The envoys of Agga, the son of Enmebaraggesi,*
> *Proceeded from Kish to Gilgamesh in Erech.*
> *The lord Gilgamesh before the elders of this city*
> *Put the matter, seeks out the word;*
> *"Let us not submit to the house of Kish, let us smite it with weapons."*

However, the elders preferred peace at any price, and advised Gilgamesh to "submit to the house of Kish; let us not smite it with weapons". The hero then went to the "convened assembly of the fighting men of the city" and got from them the decision he wanted, which was to fight Agga, the son of Enmebaraggesi; whereupon, says the ancient writer, "his heart rejoiced, his spirit brightened".[1]

There are a considerable number of tablets and temple inscriptions, mostly religious, from which a certain amount of political-military history can be painfully deciphered. But except to the philologist most of these documents are extremely dull and repetitive. Many follow a similar pattern to the one quoted above. Another example is the report of a war between the towns of Lagash and Umma. In this case the cause of the war was a frontier dispute. First it is stated Enlil, the leading god of Sumer,

> marked off the boundary for Ningursu (the patron deity of Lagash) and Shara (the patron deity of Umma) and . . . Mesilim, the king of Kish, measured it off in accordance with the word of Sataran (and) erected a stele there. (But)

[1] Kramer, S. N. *History Begins at Sumer*, op. cit.

Ush, the *ishakku* of Umma, violated (both) the decree of the gods and the word (given by man to man), ripped out its (the boundary's) stele, and entered the plain of Lagash.[1]

The king of Lagash then made war on Umma, "heaped up their skeleton piles on the plain" and, as a result, Eannatum of Lagash marked off a new boundary which was, in its turn violated by the Ummaites, who also tore up the boundary stele, drained the water from the boundary ditch, "destroyed the dedicated temples of the gods", etc., etc.

Such must have been the pattern of all the early wars of Sumer; first tribe against tribe, struggling for land; second, city-state against city-state; third, the subjugation of several states by one powerful warrior-king; fourth, imperial expansions into neighbouring countries. The same pattern can be observed in the development of earliest Egypt. If these bare chronicles were enlivened by even the briefest character-sketches of the military and political leaders, or by descriptions of the armies they led and the weapons and tactics they used, they might have more than academic interest. Lacking such details they are flat, lifeless and frankly boring.

Much more interesting are the sculptured reliefs which show us the appearance and dress of the Sumerian warriors, and the weapons they carried. Take, for instance, the wonderful "Standard" of Ur, found by Woolley. Here you see the Sumerian infantry on the march. They are a disciplined force, accustomed to drill, as one sees from the manner in which they carry their spears, all at precisely the same angle, and the fact that they are marching in step. From their heavy tunics reaching to the knees, and their long cloaks, they are evidently accustomed to campaigning in cold weather, probably in the mountains. In this they make an interesting contrast with the typical Egyptian foot-soldier who wears only a loin-cloth.

The Sumerian "mechanised" arm is mounted on war-chariots, each drawn by two asses using a very primitive

[1] Kramer, op. cit., p. 82.

harness, and carrying two men, a driver and a spearman. Fixed to the front of each chariot is a large "quiver"-like receptacle for the spare javelins. But the chariots are clumsy objects with small solid spoke-less wheels; crude in comparison with the light, graceful war-chariots of the Pharaohs which were masterpieces of the carriage-maker's art. In battle scenes the fallen enemies are depicted being trampled down by the asses; when the king returns victorious from battle files of bound prisoners are being led under guard.

With all due respect to the industry of Professor Kramer and his fellow-decipherers, I submit that such lively scenes as this, even if uninscribed, tell us more about Sumerian warfare than the repetitive tablet-chronicles with their endless, and for the most part, meaningless lists of names.

One must admit, however, that sometimes the names come to life. Statues and reliefs found at Lagash, for instance, show us the features of some of the men mentioned in the chronicles. Lagash, modern Telloh, was ruled by Eannatum during the last years before the Accadian conquest. He was a *patesi* or Governor. The first ruler of his line was *Ur-nina*, who built temples, dug canals and carried out other works of peace. Some carved reliefs show this man, depicted like an Elizabethan nobleman on his tomb, with numerous attendant children. One of these children was Eannatum, a man of very different stamp. Eannatum wanted glory, and got it. His military triumphs are commemorated in the famous "Stele of the Vultures", found by the French archaeologists working at Telloh. He took up the long-standing quarrel with the neighbouring city of Umma over water supplies, and eventually defeated the army of Umma in battle, and killed its *patesi*. Later he captured Ur, Uruk, Kish and Opis, making himself King of all Sumer. But his success was short-lived, for before long Umma rebelled, and in the struggle Eannatum was slain. His successor, Entemena, solved the problem very sensibly by digging a new canal to bring water from the Tigris to Lagash. It is still in use today, under the name of Shatt-el-Hai.

The next governor of Lagash of whom we know much was Urukagina. He threw off the yoke of Kish, proclaiming himself king of Lagash and Sumer. He is remembered for his social reforms, many of which were directed against priestly tax-gatherers. For instance a document of his period states that the High Priest may no longer

> come into the garden of a poor mother and take wood therefrom, nor gather fruit in tax therefrom.

High officials and priests were forbidden from sharing the revenues of the god between themselves, and using the temple lands as their own. Urukagina tried to protect the poor man from the rich, in cases such as that described in the parable of Naboth's vineyard. He rebuilt the sacred shrines of Lagash, only to see them destroyed in yet another disastrous war with Umma.

We owe this historical information to the French archaeologists working at Telloh. One of the most moving documents they discovered is a lamentation for the destruction of the city, and a curse on the men of Umma, who had

> shed blood on the shrine of Enlil and in the shrine of the sun-god. . . . They have carried away the silver and the precious stones and have destroyed the statue.

It ends with the words:

> Of sin on the part of Urukagina, King of Girsu, there is none. But as for Lugal-zaggesi, *patesi* of Umma, may his goddess Nidaba bear this sin upon her head!

Lugal-zaggesi, whose ugly name now appears for this first time, was another conqueror. Not content with the conquest of Lagash, he soon subdued all of southern Sumer. Transferring his capital to Uruk, he invited all the gods of the southern towns to become his patrons. We know this from inscribed ritual vases, which proclaim that the domains of Lugal-zaggesi extend "from the Lower Sea by Tigris" (i.e. the Persian Gulf) "to the Upper Sea" (i.e. the Mediterranean). If this was true the new King's reign did not last long. In about 2400 B.C. a new war-lord, more powerful and efficient than any Sumerian *patesi*, arose in the north. His name was Sargon.

Sargon was an Accadian. For some considerable time a new Semitic race, the Accadians, had been moving into northern Mesopotamia, whether by war or by peaceful penetration is still a matter for dispute. They spoke a different language, but for a long period the two races, Sumerian and Accadian, lived alongside each other in comparative amity. Sargon came from an area called Accad, a narrow strip of land where the Euphrates and Tigris converge into channels about 20 miles apart. He can claim, as one writer has remarked "to be the first dynamic leader of men to emerge from the twilight of prehistory into the full light of the written record. . . ."

Like other men of his kind, e.g. Napoleon and Adolf Hitler, he was of comparatively humble origin. He had been cup-bearer to Ur-ilbaba, governor of Kish. Nor was he ashamed of his parentage.

My mother [he writes] was humble, I knew not my father. My father's brother was a dweller in the mountain. My town was Azupirani that is set on the bank of the Euphrates. My humble mother conceived me; secretly brought me to birth; set me in an ark of bulrushes; made fast my door with pitch. She consigned me to the river, which did not overwhelm me. The river brought me to Akki, the irrigator. . . . Akki the irrigator brought me up to be his son . . . set me to gardening. During my gardening, lo, the goddess Ishtar loved me, and for fifty-four years the kingship was mine.[1]

Once again the Biblical parallel—Moses and the Princess of Egypt—needs no stressing.

How Sargon started his revolt we do not know. All we do know is that he began his military campaigns not in the

[1] Lloyd, Seton. *Twin Rivers*, Oxford University Press, 1943.

south, but in the north. Mari, Ashur, Kirkuk, Arbil were taken by his armies; next he penetrated into the Zagros mountains of southern Turkey, subduing their inhabitants. Only after he had pacified the north did he turn his chariot-wheels towards the rich and ancient cities of the south. His military skill and equipment must have been formidable for, one by one, these long-established city-states, Ur, Lagash, Eridu, Umma, Kish, Uruk fell to his sword; their power dissolved before him like grass before a prairie-fire. Soon all Sumer was his, and he was able to turn his attention to the neighbouring countries. His charioteers, spearmen and swift archers sped eastward to Persia, westward to the shores of the Mediterranean, northwards into Asia Minor. There are documents which suggest that he may even have sailed across the sea to Cyprus and added the island to his dominions.

Many centuries before the Egyptian kings of the eighteenth and nineteenth Dynasties led their armies into Syria, Sargon had established the world's first Empire. He gave a new meaning to the word "King". In ancient Sumer it had meant merely the ruler of a relatively small city-state; Sargon established himself as sole ruler of a great domain. His descendants resumed and even extended his conquests, but at last, round about 2200 B.C., the Sargonid Empire disintegrated under the combined pressure of barbarian tribes pressing in from the mountains of the east.

A period of confusion and anarchy followed, which is echoed in the famous phrase, in one of the Sumerian cuneiform tablets "Who was king, who was not king?" But in c. 2125 B.C., a new conqueror arose, ruling from the ancient city of Ur. His name was *Ur-Nammu*. At Lagash, Umma, Adab, Nippur, and Ur itself, he initiated a cultural renaissance which produced magnificent new buildings. At Ur, his capital city, he produced the greatest monument of Sumerian architecture, the temple of the moon-god, Nanna. It towered eighty feet above the Sumerian plain, and was built in three stages, rising from a base 200 feet long and 140 feet wide. Three monumental stairways led to the shrine at the top.

The period of Ur-Nammu and his successors was the "golden age" of Sumer. There was peace and economic prosperity. Art and literature flourished. Trade increased. The science of astronomy developed, and the Sumerian scribes wrote down their accumulated knowledge and wisdom on tablets which, successively translated into Accadian, Babylonian and Assyrian, passed through the Greeks and Romans into Europe. It may well have been at this time that Abraham dwelt at "Ur of the Chaldees". Many centuries later the Hebrew writers of the Bible were proud to acknowledge the fact that their Patriarch came from "The Land of Shinar".

But the end was near. In around 2000 B.C. more barbarian peoples from the east, and the Amorites of the west, pressed down in overwhelming numbers on the rich cities of the plain. This time there was no Sargon to organise them. Most likely they had become soft and over-civilised and no match for the sturdy warriors from the mountains of Persia and western Syria. So after more than 1,500 years, the material elements of Sumerian civilisation perished, though its culture was transmitted through the cuneiform tablets, first to the Babylonians, thence to the Assyrians and Persians, and eventually to the Greeks and to us.

After the collapse of Sumer a new people, led by the great Hammurabi of Babylon, were to establish themselves in the plain of Shinar, and in the more mountainous lands to the north. Babylon itself, with its fabulous tower and temples, still drew its cultural and religious inspiration from the long-dead people of Sumer. Their gods—sometimes with altered names—their temple rituals, their science, their agricultural techniques, their literature, and their writing-system, continued to be used in Mesopotamia down to the beginning of the Christian era.

But the very existence of a Sumerian people was forgotten until, by the gradual process inadequately described in this book, a succession of European and American scholars filtered, from the mixture of Persian, Assyrian and Babylonian elements, the sedimental culture of Sumer. With Ancient Egypt it shares the honour of having been the oldest civilisation on earth.

*   *   *

In some ways archaeology appears to me an inhuman occupation. The archaeologist concentrating as he must on "occupation-layers", sinking his test-pits through the compacted debris which is all that can testify for millions of individual human lives, sometimes seems like a naturalist studying the habits of termites. When, occasionally, some buried fragment of inscription, or an object found in a grave, speaks to us across the centuries of our common humanity, the scholar sometimes seems embarrassed. Yet, when we read, for example, the sombre "Lamentation over the Destruction of Ur" surely we, who have also known the misery and squalor of war, must feel a bond of sympathy.

O thou city of high walls, thy land has perished.

O my city, like an innocent ewe thy lamb has been torn away from thee;

O Ur, like a innocent goat thy kid has perished . . .

Thy lament which is bitter—how long will it grieve thy weeping lord?

Its walls were breached; the people mourn . . .

In its lofty gates, where they were wont to promenade about, dead bodies lie about.

In its spacious streets, where feasts were celebrated, scattered they lay . . .

Its corpses, like fat placed in the sun, melted away . . .

The old men and women who could not leave their houses were overcome by fire

The babies lying on their mothers' laps, like fish were carried off by the waters.

The judgement of the land perished. The people mourn.

EGYPT AND SUMER

WHICH came first, the civilisation of Sumer or that of Ancient Egypt? It is difficult to give a positive answer, since so many factors are involved. For example, Egypt was unified under one king by 3200 B.C. whereas Sumer was still divided into warring city-states by as late as 2700 B.C. On the other hand there are certain elements in Egypt's Early Dynastic Period which seem to betray unmistakable Sumerian influence. Egyptian hieroglyphic writing may be one. Another is the so-called "panelled-façade" type of architecture found in Egyptian tombs from the First to the Third Dynasties (3200 to 2800 B.C.).

These similarities are so striking as to admit no possibility of coincidence. Professor Frankfort, in his invaluable little book *The Birth of Civilisation in the Near East*[1] illustrates a number of remarkable parallels, e.g. between Protodynastic seal-cylinders found in Egypt and Iraq, and between Egyptian and Sumerian artistic *motifs* at this early period. But the most remarkable evidence of cultural connection is that shown in the architecture of the Early Dynastic tombs of Egypt and Mesopotamian seal-impressions showing almost exactly similar buildings. (See Plate XXII in Frankfort's book.)

Intrigued by these resemblances I wrote to several

[1] Frankfort, H. P. *The Birth of Civilisation in the Near East*, Williams & Norgate, 1951.

archaeologists for their opinion. Professor Walter B. Emery, Professor of Egyptology at London University, who has carried out many excavations of Early Dynastic Egyptian tombs at Sakkara, states:

> the civilisation of the *Jemdet Nasr* period of Mesopotamia and the archaic period of Egypt are apparently roughly contemporary, but the interesting point is that in Mesopotamia many of the features of civilisation appear to have a background, whereas in Egypt they do not. It is on this basis that many authorities consider that Egypt owes her civilisation to the people of the Euphrates. There is no doubt that there is a connection, but whether direct or indirect we do not know.

Dr. Margaret Murray, however, does not entirely agree with Frankfort.

> I think he is right [she says] as to the architecture in brick being of foreign introduction, though I think he is wrong in claiming that the use of mud in the form of bricks was anything but indigenous in the Nile Valley. As regards writing I disagree with him on the whole, for there were already in the (Egyptian) pre-dynastic period signs which obviously conveyed words. It is perfectly true that hieratic —the written form of hieroglyphs—was known in the First Dynasty of Egypt. It is still more surprising that all forms of Egyptian numerals were known at the same period. This seems to point to Mesopotamia as the origin of the study of mathematics. There is a great deal to be said for Frankfort's theory, but it is not by any means conclusive, but should be treated as a possibility, even as a probability, but not as a certainty.

In any case, even if this Egypto-Sumerian contact is finally proved, the question of how it was made, by what route, and whether directly or indirectly, still remains a mystery for present or future generations of archaeologists to solve.

THE SUMERIAN KING-LIST

A. THE KINGS BEFORE THE FLOOD

Name	City	Length of reign
A-lu-lim	NUN^{ki}	28,000 years
A-la(l)-gar	NUN^{ki}	36,000 years
En-me-en-lu-an-na	Bad-tabira	43,000 years
En-me-en-gal-an-na	Bad-tabira	28,800 years
Dumuzu "the shepherd"	Bad-tabira	36,000 years
En-Sib-zi-an-na	Larak	28,800 years
En-me-en-dur-an-na	Suruppak	18,600 years

Total: 8 kings, 5 cities, 241,200 years.

The Flood came. After the Flood came, kingship again was sent down from on high.

B. THE KINGS AFTER THE FLOOD

The First Dynasty of Kish

1. GA-UR	1,200 years		14. Ba-li-ih	400 years
2. GUL-la-			15. En-me-	
Nidaba-an-na	960 years		nun-na	660 years
3. (?)			16. Me-lam-kish	900 years
4. (?)			17. Bar-rak-	
5. Ba . . .			nun-na	1,200 years
6. (?)			18. Mes-za . . .	140 years
7. Ga-li-bu um	360 years		19. Ti-iz-gar	306 years
8. Ka-lu-mu-mu	840 years		20. Il-ku-u	900 years
9. Ka-ga-gi-ib	900 years		21. Il-ta-sa-	
10. A-tab	600 years		du-um	1,200 years
11. A-tab-ba	840 years		22. En-me-en-	
12. Ar-pi-um	720 years		bara-gi-si	900 years
13. Etana	1,500 years		23. Ag-ga	625 years

Total: 23 kings, 24,510 years.

The First Dynasty of Erech

1. Mes-ki-ag-ga-se ir	325 years	7. Utul-kalamma	15 years
2. En-me-kar	420 years	8. Labasher	9 years
3. Lugalbanda	1,200 years	9. Ennunadanna	8 years
4. Dumuzu	100 years	10. . . . he-de	56 years
5. Gilgamish	126 years	11. Me-lam-an-na	6 years
6. Ur-Nungal	30 years	12. Lugal-ki-aga	36 years

Total: 12 kings, 2,310 years.

The First Dynasty of Ur

1. Mes-an-ni-pad-da	80 years	2. Mes-ki-ag-Nannar	36 years
(c. 2700 B.C.)		3. Elulu	25 years
(1a. A-an-ni-pad-da)		4. Balulu	36 years

Total: 4 kings (should be five), 177 years.

The Dynasty of Awan

Total: 3 kings, 356 years.

The Second Dynasty of Kish

1. (?)	201 years	5. KU-E	300 years
2. Da-da-sig	(?)	6. . . . nun-na	180 years
3. Ma-ma-gal-la	360 years	7. I-bi-ni- . . .	290 years
4. Ka-al-bu- . . .	195 years	8. Lugal-mu	360 years

Total: 8 kings, 3,195 years.

The Dynasty of Hamasi

Hadanish 360 years

Total: 1 king, 360 years.

The Second Dynasty of Erech

En-uk-du-an-na 60 years

Total: Kingship lasted 120 years. They ruled 480 years.

The Second Dynasty of Ur

Total: 4 kings, 108 years.

The Dynasty of Adab

Lugal-an-ni-mu-un-du 90 years

Total: one king, 90 years.

The Dynasty of Mari

Total: 6 kings, 136 years.

The Third Dynasty of Kish
KU-BAU (a woman wine-seller) 100 years

(NOTE. Many of the above dynasties must have been more or less contemporary, but we know nothing decisive about them. From this point onwards the amount of overlap can be better checked and the dynasties are therefore put in parallel columns.)

The Dynasty of Akshak (c. 2600 B.C.?)		Governors of Lagash (c. 2600 BC?)	
Unzi	30 years	Ur-Nina	30 years
Undalulu	6 years	Akurgal	
Urur	6 years	Eannatum I	
Puzur-Sahan	20 years	Enannatum I	
Ishu-il	24 years	Entemena (c. 2500)	
Gimil-Sin	7 years	Enannatum II	
		Enetarzi	
		Enliarri	
		Lugal-anda	
		Urukagina (c. 2380)	

The Dynasty of Agade (Akkad)		The Fourth Dynasty of Kish	
Sargon (c. 2380)	55 years	Puzur-Sin	25 years
Rimush	9 years	Ur-Ilbaba	6 years
Manishtusu	15 years	Zimudar	30 years
Naram-Sin	55 years	Usi-watar	6 years
Shargalisharri	24 years	Ishtar-muti	11 years
"Who was King, who was not King?"		Ishme-Shamash	11 years
		Nannia	3 years

The Third Dynasty of Erech
Lugal-zaggisi 25 years

Governors of Lagash	The Dynasty of Gutium (c. 2228 B.C.)		The Fourth Dynasty of Erech	
Ur-Bau	Imta	3 years	Urinigin	7 years
Nam-makhni	Inkishu	6 years	Ur-gigir	6 years
Ur-gar	Nikillagab	6 years	Kudda	6 years
Dar-azag	Shulme	6 years	Puzur-ili	5 years
Lu-Bau	Elulumesh	6 years	Ur-Babba	6 years
Lu-Gula	Inimabakesh	5 years		
Gudea	Igeshaush	6 years		
Ur-Ningirshu	Iarlagab	15 years		
Ur-lama	Ibate	3 years		
	Iarlagash	3 years		

Kurum	1 year
...	3 years
...	2 years
Irarum	2 years
Ibranum	1 year
Hablum	2 years
Puzur-Sin	7 years
Iarlaganda	7 years
...	7 years
Tirigan	40 days

The Third Dynasty of Ur

Ur-Nammu	
(*c.* 2112)	18 years
Dungi	47 years
Bur-Sin	9 years
Gimil-Sin	9 years
Ibi-Sin	25 years

The Fifth Dynasty of Erech

Utu-khegal	
(*c.* 2120)	7 years

The Dynasty of Isin

Ishbi-Irra (*c.* 2021)	32 years
Gimil-Ilishu	10 years
Idin-dagan	21 years
Ishme-dagan	20 years
Libit-Ishtar	11 years

The Dynasty of Larsa

Gungunum	27 years
Abi-sare	11 years
Sumu-ilu	29 years
Nur-Adad	16 years
Sin-idinnam	6 years
Sin-eribam	2 years
Sin-iquisham	5 years
Silli-Adad	1 year

The First Dynasty of Babylon

Sin-muballit	29 years
Hammurabi	43 years
(*c.* 1783)	

The Elamite kings of Larsa

Warad-Sin	12 years
Rim-Sin	61 years

INDEX TO SCRIPTURAL
QUOTATIONS

(referring to Sumer, Babylonia and Assyria)

BIBLIOGRAPHY

The layman, confronted with the bibliographies in many standard archaeological works, tends to become confused by a proliferation of learned names and titles, which give him little guidance on where to look for information on any specific subject. Having frequently suffered from this difficulty myself, I have tried, in the following list, to separate books into broadly definable categories; e.g. General Works, Excavation Reports on particular sites, Art, Literature and so on. This is not to suggest that one can categorise all such books in readily classifiable compartments; obviously there must be some overlapping. Nevertheless it is possible to separate books of mainly antiquarian interest from more recent works; books on philology and linguistics from those on archaeology; and overall surveys of areas and cultural periods from fine-focused studies of particular sites. I have also tried to include representative works by archaeologists of several nations. Except in the case of Excavation Reports, which are presented under titles, the author's name is given first, followed by the title of the work, the date—and, in most cases, the place of publication.

L. C.

General Works

Cambridge Ancient History, Vol 1 (Egypt and Babylon). Cambridge University Press, 1924.

Childe, Gordon. *New Light on the Most Ancient East*. Kegan Paul, 1934.

De Genouillac, H. *Premières Recherches Archéologiques à Kich*. Paris, 1934.

Delaporte, Louis. *Les peuples de l'Orient mediterraneen (1) La Proche— Orient asiatique*. Paris, 1938.

Frankfort, H. D. *Ancient Oriental Civilisations*.

Frankfort, H. D. *The Birth of Civilisation in the Near East*. Williams & Norgate, 1951.

Gadd, C. J. *The Stones of Assyria*. Chatto & Windus, 1936.

Gadd, C. J. *The Fall of Nineveh*. British Academy: Oxford University Press, 1923.

King, L. W. *A History of Babylonia and Assyria*. Chatto & Windus, 1910.

King, L. W. *A History of Sumer and Akkad*. Chatto & Windus, 1910.

Lambert, Maurice. *La période présargonique, Essay d'une histoire sumériénne*—(Sumer VIII ff. 1952).

Lloyd, Seton. *Mesopotamia*. Lovat Dickson, 1936.

Lloyd, Seton. *Twin Rivers*. Oxford University Press, 1943.

Mackay, Dorothy. *The Ancient Sites of Iraq*. K. Mackenzie, Baghdad, 1926.

Martiny, A. *Die Kulrichtung in Mesopotamien*. 1932.

Meyer, Eduard. *Geschichte des Altertums* 2. Aufl. 1 2 (1909).

Pallis, S. H. *The Antiquity of Iraq*. Copenhagen, 1956.

Preusser, C. *Nordmesopotamische Baudenkmäler Altchristlicher und Islamischer Zeit*. Leipzig, 1911.

Schafer, H. *Die Kunst des Alten Orients*. 1925.

Smith, Sidney. *Early History of Assyria*. Chatto & Windus, 1928.

Speiser, E. A. *Mesopotamian Origins*. University of Pennsylvania Press, 1930.

Wigram, W. A. *The Cradle of Mankind*. A. & C. Black, 1914.

Wiseman, D. J. *Illustrations from Biblical Archaeology*, Tyndale Press, 1959.

Woolley, Sir Leonard. *Dead Towns and Living Men*. Oxford University Press, 1920.

Woolley, Sir Leonard. *The Sumerians*. Clarendon Press, 1928.

Early Travellers and Explorers

Buckingham, J. S. *Travels in Mesopotamia*. Henry Colburn, 1827.

Budge, Sir E. Wallis. *By Nile and Tigris*. John Murray, 1920.

Hilprecht, H. V. *Explorations in Bible Lands*. T. & T. Clark, 1903.

Hilprecht, H. V. *The Excavations in Assyria and Babylonia*. University of Pennsylvania, 1904.

Layard, A. H. *Nineveh and its Remains*. John Murray, 1849.

Loftus, W. K. *Travels and Researches in Chaldaea and Susiana*. Nisbet, 1857.

Valle, Pietro della. *Suite des Fameux Voyages de Pietro della "Valle"*. Paris, 1663.

Place, V. *Ninivé et l'Assyrie*. Paris, 1867.

Rawlinson, George. *A Memoir of Major-General Sir Henry Creswicke Rawlinson*. Longmans, 1898.

Rich, C. J. *Narrative of a Residence in Koordinstan by the late Claudius James Rich, Esq.* London, 1836.
de Sarzec. *Decouvertes en Chaldée.* Paris, 1884.

Religion

Bottéro, Jean. *La religion babylonienne.* Paris, 1952.
Contenau, Georges. *La divination chez les Assyriens et les Babyloniens.* Paris, 1940.
Ebeling, E. *Quellen zur Kenntnis der babylonischen Religion.* Berlin, 1915.
Gadd, C. J. *Ideas of Divine Rule in the Ancient East.* (The Schweich Lectures, 1945.) Oxford University Press, 1948.
Hooke, S. H. *Babylonian and Assyrian Religion.* Hutchinson, 1953.
Jean, C. F. *La Religion Sumérienne.* Paris, 1931.
Kramer, S. N. *Sumerian Mythology.* Philadelphia, 1944.
Langdom, S. *Semitic Mythology.* Oxford University Press, 1931.
Moortgat, A. *Tammuz. Der Unsterblichkeitsglaube in der altorientalischen Bildkunst.* Berlin, 1949.
Schrader. *Die Keilinschriften und das Alte Testament.* 3 Aufp. Berlin, 1903.
Van Buren, E. D. "The Sacred Marriage in Early Times in Mesopotamia", *Orientalia*, N.S. 13, 1944.

Art

Contenau, George. *Manuel d'archéologie orientala.* Paris, 1927.
Frankfort, H. *Cylinder Seals. A Documentary Essay on the Art and Religion of the Ancient Near East.* Macmillan, 1939.
Frankfort, H. *The Art and Architecture of the Ancient Orient.* Penguin Books, 1954.
Moortgat, A. *Fruhe Bildkunst in Sumer.* Leipzig, 1935.
Meissner, Bruno. *Grundzuge der babylonisch-assyrischen Plastik.* Berlin, 1914.
Parrot, Andre. *Ziggurats et Tour de Babel.* Paris, 1949.
Ward, W. H. *The Seal Cylinders of Western Asia.* Washington, 1910.
Woolley, Sir Leonard. *The Development of Sumerian Art.* Faber & Faber, 1935.
Zervos, C. *L'Art de la Mésopotamie.* Paris, 1935.

Literature

Ancient Near Eastern Texts, edited by J. B. Pritchard. Princeton University Press, 1955.
Dhorme. *La littérature babylonienne et assyrienne.* Paris, 1937.
Falkenstein, A. *Zür Chronologie der sumerischen Literatur*, 1953.

Jean, Charles-F. *La littérature des Babylonniens et des Assyriens*. Paris, 1924.

Kramer, S. N. *History Begins at Sumer*. Thames & Hudson, 1958.

Langdon, S. *The Babylonian Epic of Creation*. Clarendon Press, 1923.

Thompson, R. Campbell *The Epic of Gilgamesh* (translation). Oxford University Press, 1930.

Weber, Otto. *Die Literatur der Babylonier und Assyrer*. Berlin, 1907.

Excavation Reports

"A short investigation of the Temple at Al 'Ubaid" by P. Delgougaz (*Iraq*, V. 1938).

Ausgrabungen des Deutschen Forschungsgemeinschaft in Uruk-Warka by Heinrich, Falkenstein, Lenzen, Ziegler and Andrae. Berlin, 1936–53.

Die Archaischen Ischtar-Tempel by W. Andrae. Leipzig, 1922.

Epoque d'Ur IIIe dynastie et de Larsa by H. de Genouillac. Paris, 1936.

Excavations at Arpachiyah, Iraq by M. E. L. Mallowan. (Vol 11, Part 1), 1935.

"Excavations at Khafeje," *Bulletin of the Oriental Institute, Chicago.*

"Excavations at Nippur," *Bulletin of the American School of Oriental Research.*

Excavations at Nippur by C. S. Fisher. Philadelphia, 1905.

"Excavations at Tell el Obeid" by Sir Leonard Woolley (*Antiquaries Journal*, IV, 1924).

Excavations at Tepe Gawra by E. A. Speiser. Philadelphia, 1935.

Excavations at Ur by Sir Leonard Woolley. Ernest Benn, 1954.

Fara (Shurrupak) by E. Heinrich and W. Andrae. Berlin, 1931.

Fouilles de Telloh 1; Epoques présargoniques by H. de Genouillac, 1934.

"Report on the excavations at Jemdet Nasr, Iraq" by E. Mackay (*Field Museum of Natural History, Anthropology, Memoirs 1, 3*).

Report on the Excavations of the 'A' Cemetery at Kish by E. Mackay. Chicago, 1925.

"Tell Asmar, Khafaje and Khorsobad" by H. Frankfort (*Oriental Institute Communications,* No. 16. Chicago, 1933).

Tell Halaf, a new culture in oldest Mesopotamia by Baron Max von Oppenheim. C. P. Putnams, 1933.

"Tell Hassuna" by Seton Lloyd and Fuad Safar (*Journal of Near Eastern Studies IV, 1945*).

Tello. Vingt campagnes de fouilles (1887–1933) by A. Parrot, Paris, 1948.

The Excavations in Assyria and Babylonia by H. V. Hilprecht, Philadelphia, 1904.

The Excavations at Kish by S. Langdon. Luzac, 1925.

"The New Nippur Excavations" by McCown, Steele, and Kramer (*University of Pennsylvania, University Museum Bulletin XVI 2, 1951*).

The Temple Oval at Khafajah by P. Delgougaz. Chicago, 1940.

Ur and Eridu; British Museum Excavations of, 1919 by H. R. Hall. Methuen, 1930.

Ur Excavations; the Royal Cemeteries (2 volumes) by Sir Leonard Woolley. Oxford University Press, 1934.

"Uruk, Warka; Preliminary Reports" by Julius Jordan (*Transactions of the Prussian Academy of Science, 1930*).

For comprehensive details of excavation reports on other Sumerian and Babylonian sites, see "The Antiquity of Iraq" *by S. A. Pallis. Copenhagen, 1956.*

INDEX